TOM BASDEN

Tom Basden's other plays include *Holes* (Edinburgh Festival Fringe/Arcola Theatre, London); *There is a War* (as part of the Double Feature season in the Paintframe at the National Theatre); *Joseph K* (Gate Theatre, London) and *Party* (Fringe First Winner; Edinburgh Festival Fringe/Sydney International Festival/Arts Theatre, London). He has written for some of Britain's best comedies, including *Peep Show*, *Fresh Meat*, *The Wrong Mans* and *Plebs*, which won Best New Comedy at the British Comedy Awards 2013 and Best Scripted Comedy at the RTS Awards 2014. Tom is also a member of sketch group Cowards, who wrote and performed their own TV series on BBC4. For Radio 4 he has made two series of *Cowards* and three series of his sitcom *Party*, based on his 2009 play. Tom has been nominated for a BAFTA three times, and has won a Fringe First and an Edinburgh Comedy Award.

Other Titles in this Series

Tom Basden

THE CROCODILE

Based on a short story by
Fyodor Dostoyevsky

NICK HERN BOOKS

London
www.nickhernbooks.co.uk

A Nick Hern Book

The Crocodile first published as a paperback original in Great Britain in 2015 by Nick Hern Books Limited, The Glasshouse, 49a Goldhawk Road, London W12 8QP

The Crocodile copyright © 2015 Tom Basden

Tom Basden has asserted his right to be identified as the author of this work

Cover image: © istockphoto.com/srckomkrit

Designed and typeset by Nick Hern Books, London
Printed in the UK by CPI Group (UK) Ltd

ISBN   978 1 84842 438 8

The Crocodile was first performed on 13 July 2015 at the Pavilion Theatre, Manchester, as part of Manchester International Festival. The cast was as follows:

ZACK	Simon Bird
MR POPOV, *etc*.	Marek Larwood
IVAN	Ciarán Owens
ANYA	Emma Sidi

Director	Ned Bennett
Designer	Fly Davis
Lighting Designer	Joshua Pharo
Sound Designer	Tom Mills
Movement Director	Tom Jackson Greaves
Casting Director	Sophie Parrott
Costume Supervisor	Jessica Knight
Production Manager	Ned Lay
Deputy Production Manager	Grace Craven
Stage Manager	Fiona McCulloch
Deputy Stage Manager	Charley Sargant
Producers	Manchester International Festival and The Invisible Dot Ltd

The Crocodile was commissioned by Manchester International Festival

'Yes, I will always do what I want. I will never sacrifice anything, not even a whim, for the sake of something I do not desire. What I want, with all my heart, is to make people happy. In this lies my happiness. Mine! Can you hear that, you, in your underground hole?'

Nikolai Chernyshevsky
What Is to Be Done?, 1863

8

Characters

IVAN MATVEITCH, *jobbing actor, thirties*
ZACK, *his best friend, thirties*
ANYA, *Zack's girlfriend and Ivan's ex, thirties*
MR POPOV
ZLOBIN
SASHA IVKIN
ANDREW FRAMPTON
MR POBORSKY
DIMITRI
WAITER
PROTESTER
BARON BORIS BOGOLEPOV
TSAR ALEXANDER II

*all played by the same
actor in different hats*

Setting

A zoo in St Petersburg. 1865.

There are various animals dotted around the stage: birds in cages, a snake on a branch in a glass case, and, stage right behind a low barrier, a huge, still crocodile.

At the back of the stage are some posters for 'Extraordinary Wild Animals!' and some red curtains.

Far stage left a piece of tinsel is tied between two poles.

This text went to press before the end of rehearsals and so may differ slightly from the play as performed.

Scene One

Animal noises. Slowly merging with the sound of a crowd,
cooing and laughing. Lights fade up on the empty stage.

IVAN (*off*). I mean, what is the world coming to!? Genuinely!

    IVAN, *in a tweed hacking jacket, enters mid-flow,*
    declaiming to a seemingly imaginary audience. He is
    followed by ZACK.

    When *this* is the cultural sensation of the age? When this
garbage is what passes for entertainment? Some caged
cretins napping and pooing! I mean, what are these people
doing here? What are they expecting these animals to
actually do?

ZACK. They're not expecting anything, Ivan, they've just not
    seen them before –

IVAN. Oh, this is the end of days! You mark my words. This
    year will go down in history as the very nadir of human
    civilisation –

ZACK. You said that last year as well –

IVAN. And we've got worse, haven't we? We've fallen further
    and fouler! You know why that Darwin bloke worked out we
    came from these fluffy fucks? You know why that's
    happening *now*? Because we're turning back in to them,
    mate. We're devolving. Pretty soon we'll grow fur and tails
    and beaks and scales and waddle into the sea and turn back
    into shells.

ZACK. Yup. Did you actually read Darwin's book?

IVAN. I, yes, I read the back.

ZACK. Okay, well, either way, please don't get angry with me
    about it –

IVAN. I'm not angry with *you*, Zack, I'm angry in general. I'm an artist. That's my job.

ZACK. I is it – ?

– audience gesture

IVAN. I'm angry that the masses lap up this crap! I'm angry about how much it cost to get in here. And, to be honest… I'm still angry that all my friends go out for dinner last night and don't think to invite me!

ZACK. Oh my God, Ivan, please…

IVAN. I mean, how can that happen?!

ZACK. It was an accident –

IVAN. I felt like a goon!

ZACK. I know, I'm sorry –

land
– utter dislike

IVAN. An absolute bloody goon! Plodding past the window with Nikolai Dudin, seeing you, Anne, Pav, Sonya, Andrei polishing off dessert, and Nikolai's like 'Aren't those your friends, Ivan?' and I'm like 'Er… yes, Nikolai, they are – '

ZACK. We couldn't get hold of you –

IVAN. Horseshit!

ZACK. You weren't at home –

IVAN. I'm an actor, Zack, I am always at home!

ZACK. It… okay, look, Ivan… there was a reason you weren't at dinner, that, we… we wanted to –

IVAN. Do you know what I ate last night?

ZACK. Well, no, clearly not –

IVAN. Cheese and turnip.

ZACK. Right, that's… as in?

IVAN. Some cheese and then a turnip. It's not even a meal. It's never even been a meal.

ZACK. Well, okay, you can't pin that on us –

IVAN. I don't like being left out. Ever!

ZACK. It was, yes and I'm saying you weren't left out, per se, it was, we were talking about you, Ivan, about your shows and…

IVAN. Then you bring me here! Rub my face in this shit!

ZACK. I'm not… what? Rubbing your face in what?

IVAN. This is what's stealing my bloody audience, mate! This bilge. These… (*Points at the cockatiel*.) lightweight prats. It's a knife in the nuts bringing me here, it really is…

ZACK. Okay, well I didn't know that, Ivan. I didn't know you were in competition with animals now –

IVAN. I'm in competition with everything, man! And whether I like it or not, and I don't, this the future of showbiz. Right here. Dancing dogs, weird fish, cross-eyed cats. This'll be the only toss in town before too long, I kid you not. Survival of the bloody blandest. That's what they want… *to audience*

ZACK. I'm sorry you don't like it here, Ivan, I had no idea that zoos make you angry now as well. We can go and get a coffee once Anya gets here if you'd rather do that.

Beat. IVAN *calms down a bit.*

IVAN. What about my shows? You said you were talking about my shows. At dinner. What about them?

ZACK. Yes. And this is, I don't want to talk about it while you're… het up –

IVAN. I'm not. I've het down now. What were you saying about them?

ZACK. Yeah, okay, look, it wasn't just that we couldn't get hold of you last night, it was more that… we didn't. The truth is Ivan, we, not just me, Pavel, Anya, a few of us, thought we should talk about you and… your work and, first up, you should know, we all think you're amazingly resilient, how you've kept plugging away all these years despite uh, everything –

IVAN. Uh-huh –

ZACK. But the thing is, we, not just me, felt that it had got to the point where we had to… say something.

IVAN *nods. Beat. A little smile.*

IVAN. You don't…

ZACK. Well… really?

IVAN. I don't do it for praise, Zack.

ZACK. Oh. No, what?

IVAN. I'm just a guy.

ZACK. Yes, I know, sorry, I mean it's not that, it's more the, the other –

IVAN. Say no more…

ZACK. No, I, I think I have to –

IVAN. You'll embarrass me –

ZACK. We think you should stop, Ivan. With the shows. We think it's time you… didn't do them. That was the… what we were talking about.

Long beat.

IVAN. Okay, well, one, no. And two, what?

ZACK. We know you've been finding it tough, money-wise, and –

IVAN. The work is its own reward.

ZACK. Okay. But it's not though, is it?

You're eating cheese and turnip –

IVAN. Yeah, by choice. I like cheese and turnip.

ZACK. Okay. That wasn't the impression you gave me just now –

IVAN. Yes, it was.

ZACK. But, look, that's not the – we think it's maybe… bad for you –

IVAN. The turnip isn't –

ZACK. No, not –   IVAN. Keeps me regular –

ZACK. The work, Ivan. You have to admit, you've become a lot more bitter recently. About people younger than you, people getting more attention than you, about circuses, zoos now, you sound, well… paranoid.

IVAN. Has Anne been saying this? *First time to look back at zack*

ZACK. Anya, all of us are worried about you, Ivan, yes. That's all this is. *irritated*

IVAN. Well… okay, don't. Don't worry –

ZACK. And there comes a point where you have to accept that you gave it a good old go, but it's just not going to happen for you. And that's fine. Giving up is also, sometimes, very brave.

IVAN. Yeah, look, Zack, I know I'm hard-up and tired and, yes, okay, intense, at times. I'm not *buoyant*, like you. I'm complicated. And you're more, not simple but… simpler –

ZACK. Okay, great –

IVAN. We're fundamentally different creatures. Is what I'm saying. I'm a lion, and you're a, you know, a cow. They're both equally good, they're just different – *stress* *walk away from zack*

ZACK. Lions are clearly better –

IVAN. And when you're a lion, as I am, you've got to follow your nature.

You can't just join the herd and grow udders and chew the cud –

ZACK. I don't know what this is meant to mean –

IVAN. It wouldn't work. Everyone'd be like, 'Why is there a lion on the, on your farm?' And the farmer'd be all, 'Is it definitely a lion?' and the, this passer-by figure'd be going, 'Yes, clearly it is, it's roaring and yellow and has talent and things to say – '

ZACK. I think you should abandon this metaphor now, Ivan –

IVAN. I'm not giving up, Zack! I need to perform! Regardless of what's best for me, I just must.

ZACK. Yes, and Anya felt like that at first, but then she started with the cushions and –

IVAN. I have a duty though! To the people –

ZACK. Well… very few people –

IVAN. And to the truth. And to the justice. To expose what's really going on in this country.

ZACK. Yes but, are you confident you actually… know what that is?

IVAN. Very.

ZACK. But I mean… should you be?

IVAN. The arsehole Tsar is selling Russia down the river! I cannot and will not stop until I have brought that tyrant to his bloody knees!

ZACK. I know, Ivan, you've been saying this since college –

IVAN. Yeah, right, because nothing's changed, has it?

ZACK. Well no, of course it has, he's freed the serfs for one thing –

IVAN. Oh, open your eyes, boy! They've not been freed, they've just been released into the free-market feast. Tossed into the jaws of the flesh-eating foreign fat cats. I swear, Zack, when I think about what that man's done to the serfs it makes me physically vomit.

ZACK. But you… why though, Ivan? You don't know any serfs –

IVAN. I know serfs, lad! Don't you worry about that. I've met three of them!

ZACK. You live in the city. And you hang out in cafés, wearing that bloody English hunting jacket!

IVAN. It's a hacking jacket.

ZACK. Moaning about the evil tax-dodging foreign bastards, while blithely buying up their stuff... ← *parroting Ivan = complaints*

IVAN. This was a present from my father –

ZACK. Which you asked for –

IVAN. Which I, this is a very well-made piece of clothes!

ZACK. But you must see the hypocrisy of it, Ivan... you must see that...

Beat. *tempo shift*

IVAN. Do you actually believe in me, Zack? In my work?

ZACK. I... if it's not changing anything, if you're not getting anywhere, if the audience for the last one was made up of me, Anya, and that man with the dog, then why... don't keep doing it! Don't keep getting cross with the public because they'd rather watch a bear balancing on a ball than a grown man pretending to be a potato – *really pronounced*

IVAN. I wasn't *pretending to be a potato*! Thank you. I was portraying the famine in Northern India from the point of view of the crops – it was highly theatrical. And I'm not cross with the public, I'm cross with the famine. I'm cross it happened –

ZACK. You're cross that you're not famous, Ivan. Be honest. Aren't you?

IVAN. No, I... fame is a curse and I've actively tried to avoid it.

ZACK. Well, congratulations, you've certainly managed that –

IVAN. They don't want me to be famous, Zack. Because I confront things. Because I'm dangerous. Because I have integrity. You may have heard of it. Even in the legal world...

Beat. ZACK *turns away frustrated.*

And don't describe Mr Poborsky as 'that man with the dog', please –

ZACK. He has got a dog –

IVAN. You're trying to run down my fan! Make him sound like a vagrant –

ZACK. How am I meant to describe him then? I don't know his name –

IVAN. Well… 'the retired headmaster'.

ZACK. I don't know that either –

IVAN. Or maybe 'the distinguished-looking gentleman with the limps'.

ZACK. Okay, fine! I didn't mean to… sorry, *limps*? He's got limps, plural?

IVAN. Yes. One in each leg. Hence why I often delay the start of the show while he's dealing with the stairs.

ZACK. Okay. And do you think that maybe… do you think about that?

IVAN. About what?

ZACK. The fact that, and I don't mean to be blunt, Ivan, that after eight years doing shows, your audience has more limps than paying punters.

IVAN. Do you believe in me, Zack? Cutting to the crap for a sec: do you, my best friend, believe in what I do?

ZACK. I… Ivan, that's not the –

IVAN. Do you actually like it?

Beat.

ZACK. Yes, I…

IVAN *clutches* ZACK*'s shoulder. And smiles at him.*

IVAN. Alright then.

ZACK. The early stuff with Anya, the song-and-dance stuff, was good, but, you know, it's different now, you're not getting any younger –

IVAN. I feel like I am actually… I am full to the brim of beans –

IVAN *starts doing some dance steps.* ← theatrical – revel
in own
talent
– childlike

ZACK. Everyone's settling down now. Pav and Sonya are having a baby, Andrei's moving out of the city, you're not twenty-five any more, you can't keep doing this, on your own, to a handful of people, slumming it in a tiny flat, into your forties, it's not healthy, Ivan, it's not workable…

imagined maracas

IVAN. Mm. They were good, weren't they? – realisation – laugh
remembering
– spin into line

ZACK. What… what's that?

IVAN. The shows with Anne.

ZACK. Oh, yeah, they were great. That wasn't my point though, per se –

IVAN. I've still got the maracas somewhere. Do you think she would – ?

ZACK. No. Ivan.

IVAN. Because you're right, I shouldn't be doing this on my own –

ZACK. Anya makes cushions now –

IVAN. Yeah, I mean, we can fit it in around the cushions, Zack, you can move cushions around, famously –

ZACK. She's moved on.

IVAN. You never really move on –

ZACK. She has, she's –

IVAN. She can relearn the   ZACK. We're getting married.
songs –

IVAN *starts busting out a few dance moves. And sings.*

IVAN. 'Don't fear, my dear, the war in the Crimea. We're
sending you some cheer and beer and gear from over 'ere…'
You're getting married? *Dancing with himself*

IVAN *stops. A bit floored by this.*

ZACK. Yes. I've not actually asked her yet, but, that's, you
know, where we're at, where Anya's at. We're settling down.
She needs settling. I've been meaning to tell you. To check
you were, well not *check*, but just to more, let you know,
make sure you were cool with it. *approach Ivan*

IVAN. Why would I not be cool with it?

ZACK. No, I, exactly, that's why I –

IVAN. I think it's great! This is… yes!

Hugs ZACK. *high awkward forced laugh*

I am uber-cool with it! This is just good honest… stuff!

ZACK. Thank you. Yeah. Just cos Stefan Maksimushkin said –

IVAN. Stefan Maksimushkin is full of shit! Whatever it was.
What was it?

ZACK. No, he just, he said you said to him that you thought
one day you and Anya would get back together –

IVAN. That's, no, I didn't say that. And I wouldn't want that. I
would actively hate that in fact –

ZACK. No, good –

IVAN. And not because, don't get me wrong, Anne's lovely, I
just –

ZACK. It's fine –   IVAN. She can be extremely –

ZACK. Well, you don't have to –

IVAN. Annoying. As I'm sure you now know, but that's not,
I'm saying, Stefan Maksimushkin hasn't got any front teeth.

ZACK. What's that got to do with it?

IVAN. No, nothing, I just also remembered that about him.

ZACK. And he has got front teeth, they're just replacements –

IVAN. They're fake. You shouldn't trust someone who lies about his teeth.

ZACK. He's not lying, they were knocked out –

IVAN. Sure. All I know is, I'm very pleased, if not relieved that you're marrying Anne, because a) that's one less thing for me to worry about –

ZACK. What does that mean?

IVAN. And b) thinking about it, she's been out of the game for so long now, that getting her gig-fit would take a hell of a lot of work which frankly I don't have. And time. I meant.

ZACK. Okay. Great.

IVAN. Have you got the ring?

ZACK finds the ring box in his pocket and passes it to IVAN.

ZACK. Oh yeah, it's… don't say anything, okay? When she gets here –

IVAN. Yeah, yeah, obviously…

Opens it.

Ahhhhh. Sweet.

ZACK. It's nice isn't it?   *mmm*

IVAN. Lovely. That's… all as I would say, Zack, and feel free to ignore this, is I don't think it's very 'Anya'. Do you know what I mean?

He hands it back to him. ZACK *stares at him.*

ZACK. What are you… why would say that?

IVAN. Just being honest, mate. As per.   *cross over to stage left*

ZACK *stares at it again. The crocodile owner,* MR POPOV, *in a flat cap, enters, shouting very loud.*

3

MR POPOV. OI! — *walk right up to them then line*

They spin round. Beat.

ZACK. Yes? Why are you shouting, we're just here – ?

MR POPOV. You haven't paid. Seven roubles.

    ZACK takes two tickets out of his pocket.

ZACK. No, we, here are our tickets, look –

MR POPOV. They're the wrong ones. Seven roubles.

IVAN. You're not even looking at them –

MR POPOV. I know from the colour. Seven roubles.

IVAN. Stop saying seven roubles.

ZACK. These are the ones we were given at the front –

MR POPOV. You can't buy tickets for this bit at the front. It's separate.

IVAN. What? It can't be –

MR POPOV. Hence the tinsel.

    He points at the bit of tinsel by the edge of the stage.

IVAN. '*Hence the tinsel*'? What the hell does that mean?

      mimic

MR POPOV. Separating this bit out.

IVAN. You can't use tinsel for that.

MR POPOV. I couldn't get a velvet rope.

IVAN. You can't just sub in tinsel! You may as well use a string of sausages.

MR POPOV. Seven roubles.

IVAN. Yes, we know that! You've more than made that clear. And we've already bought tickets for the whole zoo, so we're not paying again.

ZACK. Alright, Ivan, it's fine –

IVAN. And frankly, seven roubles just for this bit, is an outrage.

MR POPOV. The other one says it's fine.

IVAN. Well, the other one's wrong! The whole zoo's only, how much was it?   *(zack paid)*

ZACK. Fifteen roubles.

MR POPOV. I've got a crocodile.

IVAN. Yeah but, have you?

Turns and sees it.

Oh yeah. *unimpressed*

MR POPOV. That's got to be worth five on its own.

IVAN. Well... why?

MR POPOV. Because... the size.

IVAN. No, you see, you don't work out the entrance fee of a zoo by the size of the animals. Otherwise they'd all just be full of like... oxen.

MR POPOV. What? You're thinking of a ranch.

IVAN. No, I'm not. Don't you tell me what I'm thinking of, fish-face!

ZACK. Let's just pay him, Ivan – *2*

MR POPOV. Yes, exactly –

IVAN. No. No, sir! These people are charlatans, Zack, they have no idea about stagecraft, audiences, pricing, we are not paying again –

ZACK. It's my money –

IVAN. He's probably just some con artist going round tinselling things off and claiming they're his!

MR POPOV. I rent my own section of zoo!

IVAN. Yeah, and I'm saying, I've never heard of that happening before. We shall not blindly hand over money like idiots, okay? We're not tourists.

MR POPOV. You've looked at my animals now –

ZACK. Not much, to be honest –

IVAN. They're not your animals! Animal ownership, as a concept, is piracy –

ZACK. Well, okay, don't start on that again –

IVAN. You don't own them. You've just kidnapped them and claimed they're yours in order to make a profit.

MR POPOV. I've got a crocodile.

IVAN. No, you see, you haven't. A crocodile is a naturally occurring thing, you can't own it. Or charge for it. That's like charging people to look at… the moon.

ZACK. It really isn't –

IVAN. In principle it is –

MR POPOV. Have you ever transported a crocodile, mate?

IVAN. I mean… I'm not answering that –

MR POPOV. So no then.

ZACK. Clearly not –

MR POPOV. So come back to me when you have –

IVAN. No. I won't. I'm not doing that –

MR POPOV. Because I'll tell you now, it's extremely bloody difficult.

IVAN. So don't do it then! Leave it where it is! It doesn't want to be here, does it?

MR POPOV. Seven roubles.

    ZACK *takes out his money.*

IVAN. Put your money away, Zack! I swear on Christ's Cross that this numpty shall not get a kopeck out of us.

ZACK. It's only fourteen roubles, Ivan.

IVAN. Yeah, and that's… do you know how much my last show was? Eight. It was eight roubles. For an hour.

MR POPOV. Well, that's more. This is only seven.

IVAN. I know it's more! I wrote and performed a savagely satirical reconstruction of the Second Schleswig War, on my own, of course it was more.

MR POPOV. What? How did you do a whole war on your own.

IVAN. Yes, well, it was heavily stylised.

ZACK. He wore lots of different hats. *to popov*

IVAN. There were hats, yes –

MR POPOV. It sounds awful –

vocal doubletake

IVAN. My point is, it was not awful, it was extremely harrowing. And far more relevant than a silent reptile so… we are not paying. End of.

MR POPOV. I'm going to get Mr Frampton.

IVAN. Do it. Get Frampton. I'll happily say the same thing to Frampton.

ZACK. Who's that?

MR POPOV. The English guy who owns this place –

IVAN. Of course!

MR POPOV. Wait here. ← *walks off past audience*

MR POPOV *leaves.* ZACK *takes out the ring again.*

IVAN. See what I mean? English! These capitalist colonisers want to buy up the bloody lot…!

ZACK. How is it not very Anya?

IVAN. Huh? It's just a bit… baroque. ?

ZACK. What? What does that mean?

ANYA *enters. And rushes over to* IVAN.

Love triangle power play

ANYA. Oh, here you are!

ZACK *spins away, hiding the ring box.*

IVAN. Annie! You made it!

Anya to cross to centre

ANYA. Can I just say, I am so sorry about last night, Ivan! If it's any consolation, the chicken thing I had was, wasn't it, Zack, very stiff and you didn't miss very much at all, other than Andrei boring us to death with his bloody, whatever it's called, gangrene. *Babbly + excuses*

ZACK. I said. What we said. I told him.

pause realisation

ANYA. Right. And, it's only because we love you, Ivan, that's the only reason we're saying any of this.

IVAN. I know.

ANYA. We all love your shows so much –

ZACK. Well, Anya, hang on –

ANYA. It's entirely about your welfare and, Zack explained about your flat –

IVAN. What about it?

ANYA. That you urinate in the sink, Ivan, I mean…

IVAN. So? I have a bathroom, that's just, that's not because of the flat –

ZACK. It's more of a lifestyle thing – *dig?*

IVAN. Why are you telling her that? *growling to zack – gritted teeth*

ZACK. It came up.

ANYA. You can't go on like this…

IVAN. It's by the bed, it's a good height –

ANYA. I know more than anyone that it's a hard life to give up, Ivan. Before I found cushions I never thought I could love anything else –

IVAN. And the cushions are great, Anne –

ZACK. They really are. We all love the cushions. And they're selling, aren't they?

ANYA. My family have bought some, yes, Zack's bought a few, and I am just a lot happier now, Ivan, look at me, and I would love you to find something you could get in to… be it clocks or jams or whittling –

IVAN. I'm an artist, Annie. You know me. Artist is all I can do.

ANYA *takes his hand and smiles at him.* ZACK *bristles.*

ANYA. Oh, Ivan…

ZACK. You used to work in a shoe shop. You could do that –

IVAN. I was shit at it though. At shoes.

ZACK. How can you be shit at shoes?

IVAN. Well, napping, et cetera, bad, you know, lacing and… manners.

ANYA *notices the crocodile behind him and screams.*

ANYA. Ahh! What is that? What the hot fuck is that?

IVAN *pulls her in for a hug.*

IVAN. It's okay!

ZACK. Oh, yes, it's a crocodile.

IVAN. I've got you… you're safe.

ZACK. It's a river-dwelling African reptile.

ANYA *gets away from* IVAN *and has a look at it.*

ANYA. Oh my God, it's extraordinary!

ZACK. It, yes, I suppose it is.

IVAN. It's fine.

ANYA. Look at its mouth…!

IVAN. It's got a big mouth, sure. So what? It doesn't mean anything, it's not, you know, moving.

ANYA. Well, it can't really, can it? In that little pit. That is my one beef with this place actually, it's so cramped. Some of the snakes back there are in, honestly, tubes –

ZACK. I'm sure's he's okay.

IVAN. Well, they only care about profits, Anne, that's why. These zoos are run by total sharks, and to be clear, I do mean people. Saving space, cutting corners, bollocks to how bored the beasts are.

ANYA. Oh, it's awful. He's catatonic, look –

ZACK. I think that's just his vibe.

IVAN. He's as sad as sin, man! Look at him –

ANYA. He really is, Zack. He looks dead –

ZACK. That's how they hunt –

IVAN. He's dead! I bet he's dead. I bet that crook's popped in a dead one –

ZACK. He's not dead.

ANYA. He hasn't blinked for ages.

IVAN. Aha!

ZACK. Again, I think that's what they do. I think crocodiles don't blink.

IVAN. Oh right, crocodiles don't blink! What next, tigers don't... shit? *Anya giggles (not for Z in scene 2)*

ZACK. Well no, I think they do –

ANYA. He's got glass eyes.

slows down

IVAN. He's stuffed! It's a stuffy!

ZACK. It's not stuffed. It's just still –

ANYA. Too still.

IVAN *leans in.*

IVAN. Oi, Croccy! Are you dead or what?

speeds up

more + more + fast + hysteric

ZACK. Ivan, stop it…

IVAN (*sings*). Croccy, are you dead? Croccy, Croccy, are you dead?

ANYA is enjoying this. IVAN plays up to it.

ANYA. Oh, Ivan, really…

ZACK. Don't waggle your hands at it!

IVAN lifts his legs into the pit. ANYA's laughing.

IVAN. Watch this, Anne! Want a nibble of my brogues then, you dead dickhead?

ANYA. Oh my God, you're mad!

ZACK. Ivan, stop it, seriously –

IVAN. It's not real, Zack! It looks totally fake when you actually get close to the –

There is a blood-curdling roar as the crocodile's mouth swings open and he swallows IVAN whole. Lights flicker. IVAN screams. As do ANYA and ZACK, leaping away from the pit.

Ah!!!! Help! Help me!

ZACK runs over and grabs his hands.

ANYA. Pull him out! — *against wall scared*

ZACK. I know, I'm trying, I'm trying!

~~ANYA runs to the side of the stage.~~ *shouts/falls*

ANYA. Help!!! Someone, help!!!

And back to IVAN. IVAN lets go of ZACK and tries to hold open the crocodile's jaws. He slowly sinks inside, yelling.

ZACK. Oh God! IVAN!!!   *2*

~~ZACK runs out.~~ *IVAN's face is still visible in the jaws.*

ANYA. Shimmy out, Ivan!

IVAN. What!!?

ANYA. Try and shimmy out!

ZACK (*off*). Help!! Quickly!! The crocodile's eating someone!! *2*

    IVAN'*s face appears in the mouth again.*

runs off

IVAN. I'm too young to die, Anne!!

ANYA. You are not going to die – !

ZACK (*off*). HELP!!!

IVAN. Oh God, oh Jesus, save me… come down and save me, I… Anne… *– demand*

ANYA. We're going to get you out of there, just… hold on…

IVAN.…I love you…

ANYA. What?

    IVAN'*s face sinks into the crocodile again with a scream.*
    ZACK *runs back into the room. Followed by* POPOV,
    yelling.

MR POPOV. What's all this bloody wailing about? What's
going on?

ANYA. You have to help us – !

MR POPOV. Where's she come from? Seven roubles.

ZACK. Our friend's in the crocodile. It just swallowed him.

ANYA. He's still alive –

MR POPOV. What? What the bloody hell – ?

ZACK. The other guy… he's in there. *pause*

MR POPOV. Prove it.

ZACK. I… what? We just saw it happen.

MR POPOV. You just don't want to pay his seven roubles.

    IVAN'*s face appears in the crocodile's mouth again.*

IVAN. Slice it open! I… ahh!

    He slides back down again.

MR POPOV. What's he doing! Get out of there!

ZACK. The crocodile swallowed him.

ANYA. Slice it open!

MR POPOV. Swallowed him how? He's in a pit.

ANYA. Slice it!

ZACK. He, yes, I know, he put his legs in because he thought it was dead –

MR POPOV. It's not dead.

ZACK. No, we know that now –

ANYA. Slice it! Slice it open!

MR POPOV. Eff off. It cost me nineteen thousand roubles.

ZACK. You'll get it back –

MR POPOV. Plus the transportation costs. That was a total hose-down –

ZACK. You'll get it all back –

MR POPOV. Well, you say that, you've still not paid the seven roubles.

ANYA. We're not negotiating! Our friend has been eaten by your animal. If he dies in there, you will be in deep shit –

MR POPOV. Oh, you're threatening me now – ?

ANYA. This man works at the law courts! *points at zack*

ZACK. As a clerk – *finger up*

ANYA. And he knows about this stuff –

ZACK. Not this exact stuff but, yes, you'll be in some trouble I expect –

MR POPOV. It's his fault for putting his stupid legs in the pit…

ANYA. You can't blame customers for getting swallowed by your animals. That's your fault for not tethering them properly, isn't it, Zack?

ZACK. Again, this really isn't my field –

MR POPOV. And he wasn't a customer, he hadn't paid. He was trespassing.

ANYA. Listen here, you weirdo, you have to get him out, okay? Now! This man is a… significant performance artist!

ZACK. Well, that's not –

ANYA. And he comes from a good family, who will reward you thoroughly –

ZACK. And he's a human being, is the main thing, so, you know, you have to!   *realist*

MR POPOV. Oh, right, so the crocodile's just got to get knifed, has it?

ZACK. Yes. Obviously.

MR POPOV. To bail out that prick.

ANYA. Don't you call him a prick!

ZACK. But yes, that's the idea.   *– the prick idea!*

MR POPOV. Well, no, sorry, not happening. That's my livelihood your mate's just got in, and I'm not going to start cutting it up for his sake. Now. Seven roubles times three is twenty-one.   *realisation*

ANYA. Times three? We're not paying for the one inside the crocodile –

MR POPOV. Alright, fourteen then.

ANYA. We're not paying at all! He's going to bloody die in a minute… Zack!

ZACK. What? What can I…?

ANYA. I think you have to climb in there.

MR POPOV. Do not climb in there!

ZACK. And then what?

ANYA. And then… take steps.

back right - change hats for scene 2

MR POPOV. Right. I'm getting Mr Frampton. I mean it this time.

POPOV *exits*. ZACK *walks over to the pit*.

ANYA. Quickly, Zack!! *- takes popov place, other side*
    of pit off bridge

ZACK. I know, Anya! I know quickly!

ANYA. Open its mouth and fish Ivan out.

ZACK. Are you out of your mind? I'm not prising open a
    crocodile's mouth –

ANYA. I'll lend you my gloves –

ZACK. He'll bloody eat me.

ANYA. He may now be full –

ZACK. I said he shouldn't start dicking about near its face, I
    said that, and he didn't listen –

ANYA. So it serves him right, does it?

ZACK. Well, it doesn't serve him wrong.

ANYA. Your best friend's being eaten and you're going to just
    do nothing?

ZACK. Well, what are you going to do? You went out with him
    for four years, you've got just as much right to get in and
    pull him out.

ANYA. Oh, you want me to get eaten by a crocodile as well?

ZACK. I want… no, I don't want that, I, in an ideal world, no
    one would get eaten by a crocodile!

ANYA. Well they have.

ZACK. And he's probably dead now anyway –

IVAN/CROCODILE. I'm not dead!!! *immediate*

    They turn and run back to the edge of the pit.

ANYA. Ivan! Are you okay in there?

IVAN/CROCODILE. I think I'm lodged!!!

ANYA. Oh, thank God. Can you hold on for a while, do you think?

IVAN/CROCODILE. Maybe, I… I don't want to die…!

ANYA. Are there enzymes in there, Ivan?

IVAN/CROCODILE. What?

ANYA. Are there enzymes trying to break you down…?

IVAN/CROCODILE. I don't know. If there are, they've not managed it yet! Thank God for the hacking jacket! Zack?

ZACK. Yes. I heard you. We're going to get you out of there, Ivan.

IVAN/CROCODILE. Quickly… it's all dark and smelly!

ANYA. Can you open his mouth from the inside, Ivan…?

IVAN/CROCODILE. I don't think so. My arms are stuck so I'd have to do it with my face, which is obviously a bit risky. From an acting point of view.

ANYA. Yes, of course.

IVAN/CROCODILE. And overall safety point of view. Please just get a person!!

ZACK. Yes we will, Ivan, we'll… I'll go to the police –

ANYA. I'll go to the press.

ZACK. What? No –

ANYA. Ivan's been eaten alive, this is a huge story, Zack –

ZACK. Get a vet! He needs a vet, not the bloody press…

IVAN/CROCODILE. Arrrgggg…!!!

ZACK. Just hold on, Ivan…

As IVAN *screams, the crocodile opens its mouth and the scream becomes a loud roar.* ZACK *and* ANYA *run out of the room in different directions. We follow* ZACK *straight into…*

[handwritten: Zack - patronising]
[handwritten: Zlobin - uninterested]

Scene Two

[handwritten margin: speed contrast]

ZACK *sits opposite* ZLOBIN (POPOV *in a Russian official's hat*), *files on his desk.* ZLOBIN *squeezes a tangerine. Beat.*

ZLOBIN. Right.

ZACK. But he's stable.

ZLOBIN. Yes.

ZACK. For now. There are enzymes, but –

ZLOBIN. What?

ZACK. Enzymes.

ZLOBIN. Oh right.

ZACK. Inside the crocodile.

ZLOBIN. Wow.

[handwritten: looks away to himself]

ZACK. But he's wearing a hacking jacket.

ZLOBIN. Great. *[handwritten: unimpressed]*

ZACK. So I think that's not a problem.

ZLOBIN. Yes. I didn't understand any of the stuff about enzymes.

ZACK. Yeah, don't worry, that's not important really – *[handwritten: patronising?]*

ZLOBIN. There's a man in a crocodile?

ZACK. Yes.

ZLOBIN. That's the gist?

ZACK. It is, yes.

[handwritten margin: pause]

ZLOBIN. Okay. Well, I've made a note of that.

ZACK. Good. Um... so obviously, we need to think about how to get him out. *[handwritten: long pause]*

ZLOBIN. Yes. Uh. I guess... let me see if my predecessor ever had one of these.

He flicks through some files.

ZACK. I'm pretty sure he wouldn't have –

ZLOBIN. She! *judge – misogeny*

(*Looks.*) Uh… nothing under crocodile. *walk back to Z*

ZACK. Yeah. So I think, we could maybe sedate the crocodile
and –

ZLOBIN. Worth looking under alligator? *– dragging out going back again*

ZACK. Oh right. I mean, maybe, but… still quite unlikely I'd
have –

ZLOBIN. Nothing. Sorry, you were saying?

ZACK. Yes, if we drug the crocodile and then maybe open it
up and –

ZLOBIN. Open how?

ZACK. Either just the mouth, or maybe actually cut open the
stomach and –

ZLOBIN. Oh my God!! *snaps out – horrified*

ZACK. Oh, yes, I suppose so – *irritated by zack*

ZLOBIN. Because I should say, right off the bat, the owner of
the crocodile, Mr Popov, has already been in – *hands on back of chair*

ZACK. Oh right – *← look at audience to himself*

ZLOBIN. Lovely guy. Very handsome. And he made it very
clear that he's keen for his crocodile not to be interfered with
in any way, shape or indeed otherwise. *reference popov delivery*

ZACK. Okay, but, we have to do something.

ZLOBIN. Oh completely! Completely agree. The problem, of
course, being that the crocodile is a business asset. Do you
see what I mean?

ZACK. No. *drawn out*

ZLOBIN. Well, it's his main earner, and therefore, main factor –

ZACK. In… what?

ZLOBIN. In what we do. Plus the zoo itself is foreign-owned, and we do have a commitment to foreign investors in this country that means to a great extent letting them mind their own businesses. *disapproving*

ZACK. But… he might die in there.

ZLOBIN. And he might not.

ZACK. Okay, but he will at some point. *more + more frustrated*

ZLOBIN. And so will we all.

ZACK. Yeah, no, I know that – *↙*

ZLOBIN. Hate to break it to you! *patronising*

ZACK. Yeah, but, the human, the risk to human life comes before the risk to business assets, though, surely?

ZLOBIN. Well, it's the same thing really. What's best for business is ultimately best for us. And if the reptile-displaying industry wants to remain competitive, then they will want to avoid getting members of the public stuck in their assets, and will therefore, in time, sort this out. Thank God. *side*

ZACK. Yeah. There's a man in a crocodile. *↙ stand*

ZLOBIN. *lookatz* I know that. I made a note of that. *approach, show note*

ZACK. So we don't have any time. We have to do something for him now!

ZLOBIN. Completely. And if he owned the crocodile in question of course we could and indeed, would spring into, into it, but as he doesn't, he is technically, isn't he, squatting.

ZACK. So? Does that matter?

ZLOBIN. Well, it makes it a lot slower, yes. Squatters are both legally protected, not to mention, stubborn –

ZACK. But he doesn't want to be in there.

ZLOBIN. And that's the housing situation all over. My advice would be to see if he can squat in it for another twelve years, *emphasise* at which point it would legally become his property and we can cut him out lickety-split.

ZACK. Yeah, look… is there someone else I can speak to?

ZLOBIN. Well, that's not very nice!

ZACK. I don't feel like you're taking it very seriously.

ZLOBIN. Well I am! What do you think I'm squeezing this tangerine for?

ZACK. I've got no idea –

ZLOBIN. To deal with stress! I don't even like them. This is what I do when I'm taking things seriously. So far I've only done it for murders.

ZACK. Okay, well –

ZLOBIN. So don't come in here and start telling me how to do my job. Yuri.

ZACK. My name's Zack.

ZLOBIN. Zack. I realise you're quite miffed about what's happened to your friend, but if you ask me, it's his fault for dangling his legs at the crocodile's face, and, in a way, what did he think would happen?

ZACK. Well, not this –

ZLOBIN. How do I even know he didn't do it on purpose?

ZACK. What? Why would he do that?

ZLOBIN. I don't know! People are odd, mate. That's one thing I've learnt doing this job. If you can imagine it, there'll be someone out there who's in to it. Maybe he was starved of attention as a child, maybe it's a sex thing, who cares? Point being, we can't start throwing taxpayers' money away because some pervert gets off on inserting himself into animals. How's that going to look?

ZACK. Not as bad as if you leave him in there I expect –

ZLOBIN. Cos it's our cocks on the blocks, sunshine. We make one bad move here and the press'll shit on us from every angle. I so much as point a penknife in the direction of this crocodile and there'll be animal lovers chucking pints of blood at me outside my houseboat. Your mate. Where does he live? *suspicious*

ZACK. You mean... before the crocodile? *sarcasm*

ZLOBIN. Yes. And what's he do? *sarcasm*

ZACK. He's a sort of performance artist slash actor who lives in Nevsky –

ZLOBIN. Oh my God! No, no, no, this is a perfect storm. They'll side with the crocodile. Definitely. I can see the articles now. They'll start banging on about how few crocodiles there are in the wild and how these entitled, arty wankers think they can go around inhabiting them rent-free. This is toxic, mate.

ANYA *enters, breathless.*

ANYA. Zack! *hysteric / loud*

ZLOBIN. What?

ZACK. It's okay, she's with me.

ZLOBIN. It's not that okay, it's my office –

ZACK. Is Ivan alright?

ANYA. Yes, he's fine. He's better than fine actually.

ZACK. Did you find a vet...?

ANYA. I, no, don't be angry...

ZACK. What's going on?

ANYA. I went to the press. And said about how Ivan was in a crocodile –

ZACK. Oh, for God's sake, Anya...

ZLOBIN. Ooh, now, what are they saying?

ANYA. They think it's brilliant – *point at Z*

ZLOBIN (*to* ZACK). Right, you see, I told you...

ZACK. What do you mean, brilliant?

ANYA. Everyone's talking about it! People from all over the city are flooding down to see him.

ZACK. Oh my God…

ANYA. There are queues round the block.

ZACK. Is Ivan okay?

ANYA. He's thrilled!

ZLOBIN. Are they saying what they want the police to do?

ZACK. But I mean… is he still alive?

ANYA. Yeah, he's singing. *slight pause*

ZACK. He's what?

ZLOBIN. Because it would be very useful to get a steer on that…

ZACK. He's singing? *disbelief*

The lights focus back on IVAN. *We are immediately…*

Zack + anya off back past audience
Zlobin → cross stage to owen's stage
owen → stands to play

Scene Three

Back at the zoo. IVAN/CROCODILE *is on his knees, singing, swinging his arms. There's a tube next to him now.*

IVAN/CROCODILE. Well, I'm a happy little, snappy little crocodile, I've long green tail and bright-white smile, I'm a wizard little lizard with a sense of style, I'm a funky little crocodile! Yes, ma'am, I'm a hunky little crocodile…

Thank you! Thank you very much!

IVAN *bows, and milks the crowd for a round of applause. A photographer,* SASHA IVKIN (POPOV *in a fedora) runs on from stage left with an old-fashioned, daguerreotype camera.*

SASHA. Croc? Yes, mate, this way! *sweeps accross stage taking photos*

> IVAN *tries to face* SASHA *for the purposes of a photo.*
> ZACK *and* ANYA *enter, jostling through some of the*
> *audience.*

ZACK. Excuse me… sorry… Ivan!

SASHA. You'll get your go in a minute…

ZACK. No, we're his friends…

sasha suprised puts camera on table

> SASHA *takes some more photos.*

baffled

ANYA. I actually used to go out with him.

ZACK. Yeah, I mean that's not, why are you bringing that up?

> SASHA *looks at her and then lines up a photo.*

SASHA. Can I get a quick photo? *pushes zack away*

ANYA. Oh, yes of course… *both push zack out of way*

> ANYA *poses for the camera.*   *shooed*

ZACK. Well… I mean, why?   *zack crossover*

IVAN/CROCODILE. Zack! That you?

ZACK. Yes, Ivan, are you alright?

IVAN/CROCODILE. Yeah, yeah, couple of journos came down
   and it's gone absolutely nuts!

ZACK. I mean, in there? Are you okay?

IVAN/CROCODILE. Yeah, fine. It's actually not that bad. I
   mean, it stinks like a box of bums, but it's fairly comfy.

> SASHA*'s got his photo of* ANYA.

SASHA. Cheers then, Croc!

IVAN/CROCODILE. Anytime, brother!

sat on wall to audience

> SASHA *leaves.* ANYA *bounds over.*

ANYA. Oh my God… all these people, Ivan!

IVAN/CROCODILE. Anne! Hey! I know, right!

ANYA. What's with the 'Croc' thing? Have they given you a name already?

IVAN/CROCODILE. I know, yeah! They're calling me The Crocodile Man or Croc. Or I actually came up with The Croc Monsieur, like the French toastie they do in Kemenov's –

ANYA. Oh, that's clever –

IVAN/CROCODILE. Well, it's pretty long-ball but some of the interviewers have enjoyed it –

ANYA. Interviews! Oh wow, Ivan!

IVAN/CROCODILE. Done two so far, yeah. Lovely, lovely people these journos, honestly.

ZACK. Okay, well, the police are being really difficult, and are basically refusing to do anything about it –

IVAN/CROCODILE. Uh-huh, cool.

ZACK. So I think I should get a vet, ask them to sedate the crocodile maybe, while we try and get you out –

IVAN/CROCODILE. Yeah, could you get me a coffee? | *pause*

ZACK. Sorry, what?

IVAN/CROCODILE. A coffee.

ZACK. How does that… are you drinking coffee now?

IVAN/CROCODILE. There's a pipe, look. Popov's rigged up a tube thing that goes into the croc's mouth and then we both get some. He's actually being pretty great – I think I got him wrong before –

ZACK. Yeah, I'm sure he's doing fairly well out of all this –

IVAN/CROCODILE. Just a coffee with a wee bit of cream… it'll help me sing.

ZACK. Yeah, the singing's not a priority –

ANYA. I'll get it, Ivan! That's no problem –

IVAN/CROCODILE. Thanks, my darlin'. Popov'll give you some cash –

ANYA. Okay, great, and well done again on all these people, Ivan.

IVAN/CROCODILE. Cheers, Anne.

ZACK. 'Well done'?

ANYA. It's really amazing.

to themselves

shouts back

ANYA *pops off.*

ZACK. I don't think you should be singing and dancing, Ivan –

IVAN/CROCODILE. It's just a bit of fun, Zack –

ZACK. But you might dislodge yourself, slip further down into the gut or something –

IVAN/CROCODILE. Yeah, no, that's fine, I've now secured myself in a wodge of veins.

ZACK. Mm. And, to be honest, Ivan, it's all, you know, quite disturbing.

IVAN/CROCODILE. What? What is?

ZACK. Making the crocodile dance like that. You can't see what it looks like but, it's, from out here, freakish –

IVAN/CROCODILE. People are loving it, mate.

Ivan dancing

ZACK. I really think you should just keep still until I get a vet –

IVAN/CROCODILE. There's really no rush, buddy. It's pretty peaceful in here, to be honest, in a womby kind of way –

ZACK. Okay, even so –

IVAN/CROCODILE. And I've made a bit more space by sort of elbowing his innards around a bit and punching my way into his arms. Hence the dancing.

He moves the crocodile's arms.

ZACK. Oh, God, Ivan, please stop it, it's genuinely quite disturbing.

IVAN/CROCODILE. Should have the legs going soon. I just need to stamp some of the pulpy stuff down into the feet to free up some space.

ZACK. Yes. And how are you… going to the toilet and stuff?

sat by pit (handwritten margin note)

IVAN/CROCODILE. Just doing it in here, yeah. It's not ideal, but I'm hoping he's going to… process it for me, in some way –

ZACK. Right, yeah, Ivan, this is awful –

IVAN/CROCODILE. It's a real eye-opener though, Zack. Being in here. I'm getting some great thinking done. You get a unique perspective on life from the inside of a crocodile, lad. I'm absolutely percolating with ideas.

ZACK. Yeah, I can imagine –

IVAN/CROCODILE. About life, death, animals, shows, obviously, economics, the lot. I'm finding it a very fertile atmosphere for cooking up some pretty major thoughts, which I do want to make sure I see through.

ZACK. Meaning what?

IVAN/CROCODILE. Meaning I'm getting a lot out of it. Artistically. And, being vulgar for a second, financially. Popov's charging thirty-five roubles to get in here now, thanks to little old me –

ZACK. What? Thirty-five roubles?

IVAN/CROCODILE. And he's giving me half, which, obviously, I'd rather not take, but it has been tough for me recently, cheese-and-turnip-wise, so –

ZACK. That feels like a lot of money, Ivan –

IVAN/CROCODILE. Thanks, yeah –

ZACK. To be charging I mean –

IVAN/CROCODILE. Oh, it's free for you and Anne, don't worry, you're on my VIP list. Point is, people are paying, and they're staying. And they're loving it, so… don't get the vet. Yet.

ZACK. They're not loving it, Ivan, they're just gawping at you.

IVAN/CROCODILE. Well, who knows...? *doesn't believe*

ZACK. They're rubbernecking. This isn't dignified, it's a... freak show. There's a man in a crocodile, that's why they're here.

IVAN/CROCODILE. Well, that's obviously the headline news, yes, but the songs are going down a total storm –

ZACK. But they are, aren't they, crap?

IVAN/CROCODILE. I need to thank you for that in fact. It was only you mentioning the songs I did with Anne that gave me the idea. The crowd are lapping it up, mate. Like hot... dogs. *= pause*

ZACK. Yes because, and I can't emphasise this enough, you're in a crocodile –

IVAN/CROCODILE. Once I get the old legs going, I'll really be able give them a show.

ZACK. It doesn't matter what you do, Ivan, just carry on drinking and shitting in there and they'll still be writing about it.

IVAN/CROCODILE. I haven't done one of those yet actually! *emphasise*

ZACK. Okay, good.

IVAN/CROCODILE. I've been holding it in for his sake.

ZACK. That'll go down just as well as those stupid songs.

IVAN/CROCODILE. I know the songs are stupid, Zack, I know that! They're meant to be stupid, so they're actually therefore clever.

ZACK. Right. That's lucky –

IVAN/CROCODILE. Nevertheless, this is an opportunity for me. Being in here. Which I have to take. Career-wise.

ZACK. You want to be a singing crocodile now? That's your new career plan?

IVAN/CROCODILE. It's now or never, Zack, I'm thirty-two, I can't keep doing my shows to no one, it's not healthy –

ZACK. Yes, I know. I told you that.

IVAN/CROCODILE. The songs are just the beginning! They just lure 'em in. Once I've done that, once I've got them looking, I hit them with the good stuff. Where it hurts. Get all of Russia to hear what I have to say. Show people what the Tsar's doing to us here… free their tiny minds!

ZACK. Yeah, I'm going to get a vet –

IVAN/CROCODILE. No, Zack, listen – !

IVAN *grabs his arm.* ZACK *screams.*

ZACK. That's really fucking creepy!

IVAN/CROCODILE. And calm down! I have to stay in here, mate. For the art. For the message. This crocodile is my way to get that out. It's much bigger than me. In more ways than one.

ZACK. Please let go of my arm, Ivan, this is absolutely appalling –

IVAN/CROCODILE. Being eaten by a crocodile could the best thing that ever happened to my career, Zack, and I honestly never thought I'd say that. Please do not get a vet. For one thing they're famously pricey.

ZACK. Let my go of my fucking arm, I'm going to have a panic attack!

IVAN/CROCODILE *does so.* MR FRAMPTON (POPOV *in a bowler hat*) *waddles over. He starts hitching up a banner behind him. It's for Petersham Tweed Jackets.*

MR FRAMPTON. Ivan, hi! Andrew Frampton.

IVAN/CROCODILE. Sorry?

MR FRAMPTON. Andrew Frampton. Owner of this here zoo. Really wonderful to meet you.

IVAN/CROCODILE. Oh, yeah, I've heard all about you.

MR FRAMPTON. Well, likewise! Yes!

(*To* ZACK.) Sorry, can you give us a sec?

ZACK. Oh, I'm actually –

IVAN/CROCODILE. He's with me, Frampton.

tone change

MR FRAMPTON. Oh right, yes, great.

ZACK. I'm Zack.

starts wheeling banner – funny

MR FRAMPTON. Perfect. Andrew Frampton. Well, look, Ivan, I wanted to come down to personally introduce myself and say a big hello and thank you for everything you're doing for the zoo in terms of the sheer 'being inside a crocodile' factor. It's really just wonderful stuff from our point of view and, well, I'm sure I don't need to tell you how much it's captured the public's imagination.

IVAN/CROCODILE. I'm as humbled by it as you are.

MR FRAMPTON. Well, exactly. And I thought I should let you know that everyone in the office is a huge fan of everything you're doing.

IVAN/CROCODILE. Well, that's lovely to hear.

ZACK. What's that banner?

MR FRAMPTON. Sorry?

ZACK. Why have you just put up a banner for Petersham Tweed Jackets?

MR FRAMPTON. Yes, no, I know I have, that's, I was going to say: good news! We've got sponsorship!

IVAN/CROCODILE. What? Have we?

MR FRAMPTON. From Petersham's. I've got connections at Petersham's.

IVAN/CROCODILE. I'm not cool with that, Frampton. *dead face*

MR FRAMPTON. Oh well, uh, they are sponsoring the whole zoo, not just you –

IVAN/CROCODILE. Like hell they are, mate. I'm the reason people are coming –

MR FRAMPTON. Well, of course, you are a very popular attraction, but there are many other, the penguins are –

IVAN/CROCODILE. No one gives a shit about the penguins, Frampton. They can get penguins anywhere.

MR FRAMPTON. Well, that's… geographically naive and, well, the penguins are a real favourite here –

IVAN/CROCODILE. Why is the banner not behind the penguins then?

MR FRAMPTON. Yes, no, I know. And, look, it is a nice bit of investment, so it will of course mean that we're now more financially able to help with your comfort and overall well-being –

IVAN/CROCODILE. I'm not doing free advertising, Frampton. For you and your pals back in Blighty. This is Russia, mate, you can't just turn up here with your bags of swag you've wrung out of oily faced northern factory workers and start flogging all your clobber from your Crystal Palace –

MR FRAMPTON. Well, no, it's not like that –

IVAN/CROCODILE. Who's the banner for, Zack?

ZACK. Petersham Tweed Jackets.

IVAN/CROCODILE. Never heard of them.

MR FRAMPTON. They make hacking jackets. I gather from Popov that you're wearing one.   *feels chest to check*

IVAN/CROCODILE. Oh. Yes, I am.

MR FRAMPTON. So I telegrammed a uni chum in London and he was absolutely thrilled that you like them…

IVAN/CROCODILE. Right, well, I mean, I do –

MR FRAMPTON. I've got one myself actually.

IVAN/CROCODILE. The workmanship is excellent –

MR FRAMPTON. Oh, look, it's unbeatable. And no one said anything about this being free, by the way, we want to keep

you, the talent, absolutely happy, so obviously, if there is
anything you'd like from Petersham Tweed Jackets then you
should say at once –

IVAN/CROCODILE. Can I have a Petersham Tweed Jacket?

MR FRAMPTON. Yes, of course.

ZACK. Well, what's the point of that?

IVAN/CROCODILE. There are other colours, I expect –

MR FRAMPTON. Oh, many, yes –

IVAN/CROCODILE. There you go –

ZACK. No, I mean, when you're in a crocodile –

MR FRAMPTON. And they also make top hats, waistcoats and
cravats.

ZACK. Which, again, not that useful –

IVAN/CROCODILE. And are they ethical, Frampton? As
company? Do you know?

MR FRAMPTON. Uh… I know they make tweed.

IVAN/CROCODILE. Sounds fine. I'll have all that stuff then –

MR FRAMPTON. Superb! They'll be so excited.

IVAN/CROCODILE. If it means there's more funding going to
the upkeep of the animals, then it's my pleasure…

MR FRAMPTON. Fantastic. Thanks so much for being so
reasonable, Ivan –

IVAN/CROCODILE. No problem at all, Frampton.

MR FRAMPTON. And wonderful again to meet you –

IVAN/CROCODILE. Yeah, could you get me some food?

MR FRAMPTON. Oh. Yes. What sort of…?

IVAN/CROCODILE. Well, something that can fit down the
tube so maybe…

ZACK. Soup?

shouting down zack

IVAN/CROCODILE. Caviar, I was going to say.

ZACK. Caviar?

IVAN/CROCODILE. Bit of caviar maybe. Just cos it's small, isn't it?

MR FRAMPTON. It is, yes. It's eggs.

ZACK. Do you like caviar?

IVAN/CROCODILE. I reckon I would, yeah. Probably good for the croc's stomach too, I expect, a bit of Beluga caviar…

MR FRAMPTON. Yes, that's… that is the most expensive one.

IVAN/CROCODILE. Great.

MR FRAMPTON. Okay, great.

IVAN/CROCODILE. Thanks.

MR FRAMPTON. Well no thank you, thanks so much again for choosing our zoo to… get into a crocodile in –

IVAN/CROCODILE. You're welcome –

ZACK. I don't think he chose it.

MR FRAMPTON. And nice to meet you too. There.

ZACK. Zack.

There is shouting offstage. ANYA appears at the side of the stage, by the tinsel, holding a coffee, distressed.

ANYA. It's for Ivan! It's for the Croc! I'm not pushing in!

ZACK. Anya!

(*To* FRAMPTON.) Sorry, can you, she's meant to be on a VIP list.

FRAMPTON *goes over to* ANYA *and shouts to people offstage.*

MR FRAMPTON. She is a friend of Croc's! Please calm down! You will all get your chance to see him, just… I don't care how disabled you are, you do have to wait, sir…

off stage (funny not to see)

ANYA. I've got a coffee for Ivan.

MR FRAMPTON. Yes. Please do come in.

He lets her through the tinsel. ANYA *heads over.*

ZACK. Are you alright?

ANYA. A couple of people spat in my hair cos they thought I
was barging in.

ZACK. Oh my God!

IVAN/CROCODILE. Did any of it go in the coffee?

ANYA. No, I managed to shield it.

IVAN/CROCODILE. Good girl, Anne! Be a love and pop it in
the pipe. I'm gasping.

ANYA. There was an old man back there who said he knew
you, actually, Ivan.

IVAN/CROCODILE. What? Who was that?

ANYA. With a couple of limps.

IVAN/CROCODILE. Mr Poborsky! Let him through!
Frampton! Send in Poborsky!

MR FRAMPTON. Right, yes, which one's Poborsky?

FRAMPTON exits. MR POBORSKY (POPOV *in a fur hat*)
*limps onstage very slowly. He carries a small dog (stuffed,
probs).*

MR POBORSKY. Ivan! I came as quickly as I could!

IVAN/CROCODILE. Mr Poborsky! Have you seen what's
happened? People are finally listening! Isn't it wonderful?

MR POBORSKY. Mm... I preferred the old stuff.

Beat. IVAN/CROCODILE *wasn't expecting this. Sour
atmosphere.*

IVAN/CROCODILE. Yup, let's lose Poborsky! Frampton!

He switches hats to become FRAMPTON *again, heads out.*

[handwritten margin note: dog in Frampton hat — throws dog out + puts on F hat]

MR FRAMPTON. Right, come on, off you go then…

IVAN/CROCODILE. Miserable old bastard.

(*To* ANYA.) Coffee please, Anne.

ANYA. Yes, sorry, Ivan, one sec.

She starts to pour it into the tube. ZACK *sidles over to her.*

ZACK. I'm so sorry they spat at you…

ANYA. Huh? Yeah, yeah, it's all a bit crazy, isn't it?

ZACK. I know, it's absurd. I can't wait to just get out of here –

ANYA. There are touts outside selling tickets for three hundred roubles!

ZACK. Yes. Exactly. So I've booked a table at Benoit's tonight…

IVAN/CROCODILE. Bit slower, Anne, my love!

ANYA. Sorry, Ivan.

ANYA *carries on pouring the coffee. Half-listening.*

ZACK. For seven thirty. I know you've been wanting to go…

ANYA. Yes. Sorry, who?

ZACK. No, what? It's a restaurant. *Benoit's.* The French place. You mentioned. It was starred, it's meant to be… starred.

ANYA. Oh right?

ZACK. For tonight. That's… is that okay?

ANYA. Yeah, just, obviously, if we leave we may not be able to get back in.

ZACK. Well… so?

ANYA. So everyone's desperate to get in here, Zack.

ZACK. Yeah but, that's not a reason to do it, I mean, I've booked the table, Anya, I've, we're apparently by a window. In a good way.

She's poured all the coffee now.

ANYA. Finished, Ivan!

IVAN/CROCODILE. Thanks, Anne. Don't know what I'd do without you.

ANYA. If there's anything else you want, just shout at me.

ZACK *leads her away from the crocodile.* FRAMPTON *comes in and starts spooning caviar into the tube.*

ZACK. Anya, don't... encourage him, okay?

ANYA. What do you mean?

ZACK. This is obviously, for someone like Ivan, going to have an impact, and we need to protect him a bit –

ANYA. What? What do you mean 'someone like Ivan'?

ZACK. Well, for someone as... dramatic and, Ivan's a massive show-off, Anya, this is right in his wheelhouse –

ANYA. No, he's not, he's an actor –

ZACK. I, yes, exactly –

ANYA. And performance artist –

ZACK. Yeah, again, fine, I don't really know what that is, I'm just saying, this whole circus really isn't going to help –

ANYA. It's not a circus, it's a zoo –

ZACK. It, I know, I mean, given what we decided last night, we need to make sure that all this doesn't, you know, derail that. For Ivan's sake.

ANYA. So what if it does? Maybe this changes things –

ZACK. It, no, it can't –

ANYA. This is a break for him, Zack – a weird one sure, but they all count. You've got to grab 'em when you get 'em, that's how this industry works –

ZACK. But it's not just about breaks, though, is it? That's not why we all decided to intervene –

ANYA. You said he was destitute and weeing in the sink –

ZACK. Yes, and he is, but –

ANYA. That's why you suggested it.

Behind him, the crocodile slowly begins to stand up. ZACK *takes her hands.*

ZACK. We all suggested it. In a way. I'm saying this, Ivan being in a crocodile, could be extremely bad for him, Anya. In more ways than the immediately medically obvious. And I want to make sure that we're united about how we handle it and don't get distracted by, uh… Anya?

(handwritten: Ivan starts rising)

He smiles at her. She's looking at IVAN/CROCODILE *behind him.*

ANYA. Oh my God!

IVAN/CROCODILE *is now standing.* ZACK *turns and sees this.*

ZACK. Oh shit! Ivan, are you doing that?

IVAN/CROCODILE. Big time. Ooh… that's better. *(handwritten: fully stood)*

ANYA. I mean… you're absolutely huge! *(handwritten: walks towards Ivan)*

IVAN/CROCODILE. Cheers, Anne. Finally forced my way into the legs. *(handwritten: part of lewd joke)*

IVAN *starts to move the crocodile's legs.*

ANYA. Oh wow, Ivan, that's amazing.

A journalist, DIMITRI (POPOV *in a beanie), enters.*

DIMITRI. Croc! Over here! *(handwritten: stood on chair)*

IVAN/CROCODILE *spins round to face* DIMITRI.

IVAN/CROCODILE. Yes, mate!

DIMITRI. How you feeling in there?

IVAN/CROCODILE. Better than ever, dude.

DIMITRI. Got any more songs for us?

← serious - tone change

IVAN/CROCODILE. Ha! No, no, not right now I'm afraid,
lads, it's time to get a little bit serious, if I may. For, ladies
and gentlemen, boys and girls; thank you for joining me here
this afternoon, my name is The Croc Monsieur: artist, singer,
prophet, miracle of nature, social outsider and reptilian   *pause*
                                                                               for others
insider. I am here not just to entertain you, but to help you.   *to sit.*
To save you. And I'd like, if I may, to tell you a little story.
Once upon a time, in a city not unlike this one, full of people   *slow*
not unlike you, there was a zoo, not unlike this one, full of   *down*
animals, not unlike me. The owner of this zoo looked after   —   *everyone*
his animals: he fed them, washed them and kept them   *sits*
healthy, because if they were happy, his visitors were happy,
and business boomed. And although the animals weren't
free, they appreciated the owner's care and lived in peace
with one another. One day, however, everything changed.   *plug*
Two European men in long, tweed coats, with bowler hats
and large grey moustaches (one each, that is) waddled
around the zoo discussing the political ideas of the day. They
were entrepreneurs, siphoning money that ought to be paid in
tax in their home country into developing nations like this
one. As they passed the chimpanzee cage, one man turned to
the other and said: 'Now that the king of this land has
released the serfs from their bondage, turning slaves into
citizens, is not animal captivity also shameful and immoral?'
The chimpanzees, who spoke a smattering of human
languages, quickly arranged a meeting with all the animals to
discuss what they had heard. The bigger beasts with long
lifespans, like the elephants and the hippos, thought it best to
ignore what humans were doing and focus on themselves.
The more excitable creatures, however, like the stoats and
the snakes, whipped up the other animals into a self-
righteous frenzy, and led a brash band of beasts to confront
the zookeeper and demand that this wave of progress be
extended to them. And, shamed by the animals' accusations
of tyranny, the zookeeper agreed at once to treat them in a
manner in keeping with modern, human morality. Instead of
being freed, the animals would be paid. They would stop

being slaves and become workers. They'd pay for their food and for their cages to be cleaned, but in turn they would receive a wage from the zoo. The animals accepted at once, excited and emboldened by their new rights and freedoms, and, although many of them couldn't understand how their situation would be any different, or the overall concept of money, they felt that they had won a famous victory and were filled with optimism and excitement. At first, nothing changed. Some species nibbled or widdled on these small round pieces of metal being deposited into their cage. Some ignored the coins completely, oblivious to them being brought in or taken away, uninterested in the entire transaction, and life carried on as it always had. Then, one day, the chimps began to realise that they could choose when and how to spend their money. By eating less food and refusing to have their cage cleaned, they managed to stockpile their shiny coins and, within a week, had used the money they'd saved to buy a cactus. With which, they were understandably thrilled. Two months later, hungry and dirty,

they used their savings to compile mirrors and lights and hats and kites, and added another floor to their cage, slowly turning it into by far the most eye-catching and elaborate part of the zoo. Although some of the smaller chimps died from hunger or diseases that bred in their growing pyramid of dung, soon their cage attracted by far the most visitors. The hyenas, living nearby, saw what the chimps had done and quickly followed suit – diverting the money they would have spent on food and cleaning into flashy fireworks to lure visitors over to their cage. Other animals, led by the elephants and the hippos, refused to have any part of this, unwilling to compete for attention, unmoved by the chimps' and the hyenas' sudden surge in popularity, calling it faddish and pointless, and harmful for the collective health of the

zoo. And despite their new-found popularity, the chimps and hyenas were frustrated. And felt cheated. All of the animals in the zoo were still being paid the same amount, even though the chimps and the hyenas brought in way more traffic, having invested so heavily in their own cages. And they promptly informed the zookeeper that, from now on, the

gate receipts should be divided among the animals according
to the number of visitors they receive, rather than by equal
share. By now the hyenas and the chimps were the zoo's star
attraction, and the owner couldn't afford to anger them and
had no choice but to agree to their demands. And, as money
flowed to the chimps and the hyenas, other animals began to
suffer. Over the next few months, unable to attract visitors,
the otters starved and the turtles got worms. The llamas,
who'd invested their entire budget on berets, survived
merely on the food that the elephants were willing to spare
and fire over the fence with their trunks, if that's possible.
All the while, the aspirational animals kept developing their
cages, which by now had become entire enclosures, which it
was almost impossible for visitors to avoid. The zoo itself
continued to thrive, the gate receipts soaring as the animals
developed and improved every section of the zoo by
themselves, and yet more people rushed to see the results.
Unable to see a way to be competitive, the genetically lazy
two-toed sloths took out a mortgage on their cage from a
passing bank manager and instantly became a big attraction,
spending the windfall on expensive plastic surgery to make
them look more like the chimps, and confuse the fans of the
hugely popular primates into visiting them instead. Soon all
of the animals had taken out mortgages on their cages and
spent the money on increasingly outlandish and attention-
grabbing items, and the zoo was filled with fountains and
vases, chandeliers and murals. Exactly one year after their
last visit, the two entrepreneurs with the grey moustaches
(still one each) visited the zoo once more, confused and
amazed by how it had changed. The previously well-
proportioned site was now totally overrun by the sprawling
enclosures of six or seven species who had bought up
everything and had complete and constant access to the
visitors. And in a small, squalid corner of the compound, the
remaining hundreds of species lived huddled together in a
ghetto, destitute and diseased, unseen by the zoo's many
customers. As the men passed the ninth chimpanzee cage,
piled high with gold bars, fine wines and portraits, one
turned to the other and asked: 'What's happened to this

place?' The other man smirked and lit a cigar wedged in his thick lips: 'Well, it's obvious!' he replied, puffing out a woolly web of smoke, 'What's happened here… is progress.'

draw out

Snap blackout. There is a candle lit. The lights grow onto…

Scene Four - *guy set scene (candle + glasses)*

ZACK *and* ANYA *having dinner.* ZACK *holds the ring box under the table. And he now has a tartan hanky in his top pocket.*

ZACK. I'm not the cynical one, Anya! He is. He distrusts any ideas that aren't his and only reads stuff he already thinks. He doesn't know anything about what's going on –

ANYA. It's not his job to know anything –

ZACK. He doesn't even think anything. Ten years ago he's doing shows demanding the serfs be freed because that's what's all his hip, actor friends were saying and now he comes out with this crap –

ANYA. He's allowed to change his mind –

ZACK. He's like a monkey throwing shit against a wall –

ANYA. Oh, not while I'm eating, Zack!   *over dramatic*
                                          - turn away
ZACK. You're not eating.

ANYA. Planning to eat! *picks up menu*

ZACK. And he hasn't changed his mind, he hasn't even got a mind –

ANYA. Ivan is trying to do good, Zack, that's all –

ZACK. No he's not. He doesn't care. It's not about doing good, it's about looking good.

ANYA. Well, what are you doing?

ZACK. We're not talking about me.

ANYA. How convenient. *sarcasm*

ZACK. What do you want me to do? Go around being angry about stuff? Complain about how farmers are being treated while sitting in a restaurant in St Petersburg, is that what I'm meant to do?

ANYA. You tell me.

ZACK. It won't do anything, Anya. You think these artists and students drinking coffee, banging on about Marx and revolution, are ever actually going to do anything? They're fakes. Full of fake fury. They're just afraid of actually working for a living.

ANYA. Ivan works very hard. *– looks at zack*

ZACK. He gets up at noon.

ANYA. Because he works in the evening –

ZACK. And he pisses in the sink.

ANYA. Yes, he said, it's a good height.

ZACK. Oh, that's fine now, is it? You were disgusted by that last night…

ANYA. Ivan follows his heart, Zack. That's all. As always, he is just trying to do what's right.

ZACK. Yeah, that's the problem. These idiots who think they're right all the time. Religion's got it upside down, it's not the sinners you have to worry about, they're not the dangerous ones, it's the bloody righteous. The ones who'd rather kill you than admit they were wrong –

ANYA. What do want him to do then?

ZACK. Get out of the crocodile –

ANYA. Became a clerk? Would that help? More clerks? *sarcastic*

ZACK. …get over himself and live a normal life like the rest of us.

ANYA. I don't think he can –

ZACK. Yeah, of course, he'll shrivel up and die if he's not
   being looked at – *patronising edge*

ANYA. Get out, I mean. I don't think he can. And even if he
   did, it wouldn't matter. Ivan's not like you, he needs to
   perform –

ZACK. No, right, I'm just some blob who wants to live in a box
   and never let anyone see me – *"I didn't say that..."*

ANYA. I'm not calling you a blob, Zack. Don't put words in
   my mouth. You're not a blob, you're just what actors would
   call a civilian. Unlike Ivan, and, to a certain extent unlike
   myself, you don't have a desire for attention. Or talent. And
   I'm not being horrible, that's just the way it is. You're a
   classic clerk. You're not a doer, you're a writer-downer of
   what other people do. Ivan's different. He has a calling.

angry

anya – actressy self-important

ZACK. Uh-huh. You know he's getting half the zoo's takings
   now? That's an extremely lucrative calling he's got there.

ANYA. That's not why he's doing it.

ZACK. Not to mention shit-tonnes of tweed –

ANYA. This is what he did when he didn't earn anything –

ZACK. Yeah, and he was shit then as well.

ANYA. What? Oh my God! No he wasn't –

ZACK. You thought he was shit too.

ANYA. I, no, I did not –

ZACK. Yes you did, Anya!

ANYA. I've always enjoyed Ivan's shows, as a matter of fact,
   even the bad ones –

ZACK. They were all bad! All of them. The whole thing was
   bloody awful! Seeing him afterwards, thinking up
   deliberately vague things to say. And now he happens to
   have got in a crocodile and everyone's talking about him,

you invent this whole new narrative about him actually being good all along to make sense of something totally random. *microcosm of the play*

ZACK *takes out his hanky and mops his brow.*

ANYA. You know what I think, Zack? I think you're jealous. *drawn out – land*

ZACK. Of what?

ANYA. All the attention he's getting.

ZACK. He's in a crocodile. Anyone would get attention for that –

ANYA. Yes, but not everyone did, did they? He did. He went out there and he bloody did it.

ZACK. Well, not really, the crocodile did it, he just goaded it.

ANYA. Which you were too scared to do – *drawn*

ZACK. Because I didn't want it to eat me – *not brave enough for her*

ANYA. Exactly.

ZACK. What? What do you mean 'exactly'? I don't want to live inside a crocodile, Anya! Why would anyone want that? It would be fucking horrible. You can't do anything. You can't go anywhere. You spend your whole life surrounded by people staring at you. It's a bloody prison sentence –

ANYA. And it's one that Ivan's prepared to serve, which, as someone who cares about him very deeply, I think is extremely impressive.

ZACK. What?

ANYA. To let people observe him with no thought for his own privacy –

ZACK. What do you mean you 'care about him very deeply'? What's that?   *emphasise*

ANYA. We were together for a long time –   *almost proud*

ZACK. Yeah, but you're not now.

ANYA. No, but –

ZACK. So don't tell me you still care deeply for him, that's not, how's that meant to make me feel?

angry → ANYA. It's not. Not everything's about how *you* feel, Zack.

ZACK. I know. I know that. And I care about him too. I've known him a lot longer than you have.

ANYA. So be happy for him then! Don't just turn on him the minute he becomes a success –

ZACK. How is *that* being a success? What's successful about that?

The WAITER (POPOV *in a beret*) *comes over.*

WAITER. Are you ready to – ?

ZACK. No. – *shout - not looking at waiter*

WAITER. Of course.

And backs off.

ANYA. And you say how awful it was –

angry revelation about how Zack feels about Ivan

ZACK. Can we talk about something else?

ANYA. Going along to his shows, seeing him after and everything, but it wasn't actually, was it?

ZACK. Anya, please, it doesn't matter –

through defending Ivan

ANYA. You loved it. You loved every minute of it. Seeing how empty it was, watching people walk out –

ZACK. That's not fair –

ANYA. You couldn't wait to get home and rake over all the shit bits, that's why you kept going –

ZACK. I went because he's my friend –

ANYA. For the relief. Every time it went badly for Ivan, it was a huge relief for you.

ZACK. Why would I want that?

ANYA. He's not your friend, Zack, you hate him. You've hated him for years. You only ever wanted him to fail. To embarrass himself and give up and… make cushions.

ZACK. I didn't make you do that. Anya.

She stares at him. The WAITER *begins his approach again.*

The acting wasn't working, and you'd given it a good old go and you decided, and I agreed, that you should try something else. That was your decision.

ANYA. Did you think *I* was shit? Zack?

ZACK. No. Of course not. I love you.

ANYA. Oh my God…

ZACK. You were amazing. And you *are* amazing at cushions.

ANYA. No I'm fucking not! They're not even square!

The WAITER *turns round.* ANYA *is in a bit of a state.* ZACK *takes her hand across the table.*

ZACK. I thought that was on purpose… I thought they were just… modern.

Beat.

I mean, I like them that shape.

ANYA. No you don't! They're shit. You don't like them, you just like that I'm doing that and… yours and… a nobody…

ZACK. I think the cushions have a real future, Anya. Honestly. Every single one you make is more square.

ZACK *looks down at the ring box.* ANYA *looks at the menu.*

And, I want us to think about our future. Together. Anya?

She looks up.

I've been, this has all been really tough and… I've been working a lot recently and we've not had much chance to actually talk –

ANYA. I know –

ZACK. Openly. And work out what we really want. From each other. From life.

ANYA. Yes.

ZACK. Because we've been together a long time now. And, you know, lately, I've been thinking a lot about… us and where it's all going –

ANYA (*continued*). Completely.

ZACK. And, it really feels like maybe now is the right time to finally do something about that and –

ANYA. I think it is.

ZACK. Take it to the next level.

ANYA. While we're still young. What?

ZACK. Anya.

He puts the box on the table.

ANYA. Ah, right –

ZACK. Will you marry me?

Beat. She reaches over to the box and opens it. Stares at the ring. For a while. Then puts the box down.

ANYA. Did you want an answer now?

ZACK. Well… yeah, ideally.

ANYA. I think, in that case, no. Thanks.

The WAITER *approaches again.*

WAITER. Are you ready to order – ?

ZACK. No.

WAITER. I can recommend the bouillabaisse.

ZACK. I literally just said no.

The WAITER *tries to laugh it off. He spots the ring box.*

WAITER. Oh, now… shall I get a bottle of Champagne?   *picks up ring*

ZACK. No thanks.   *signal to stop music*

WAITER. Oh. Oh… no, did she, you didn't say no, did you? Ah… shit!   *– dodgy*

ZACK. Can you piss off, please?

WAITER. Of course. Oh, mate… chin up…   *Z shakes waiter off*

The WAITER *puts a hand on* ZACK'*s head.* ZACK *wriggles it off. The* WAITER *looks at* ANYA *keenly. And walks off.*   *pause*

ZACK. It is because of the ring?   *what Ivan said!*

ANYA. No.

Beat. ZACK *takes the box and looks at it.*

ZACK. Is it a bit baroque?

ANYA. I don't know… can we not talk about it now, okay? Everything feels so weird since the whole crocodile thing.   *excuse, can't think about*

ZACK. Yeah. That was this morning ,Anya. That happened this morning.

The WAITER *comes back. Holding a newspaper.*

WAITER. Hello again, sorry –

ZACK. Can you just…? I'll call you over –   *Basil fawlty*

WAITER. Are you The Croc Madame?

ZACK. What…?

WAITER. I don't mean to, I'm sorry for hassling you, just I saw your picture in *The Gazette* and was just like, oh my God, that's her –

ZACK. The Croc Madame?   *– exasperated at himself*

WAITER. The Croc's wife.   *sad/funny - caught himself out*

ZACK. Girlfriend. Ex-girlfriend.

WAITER. Cos you're in the paper. You've got that same dress on and everything.

ANYA. I've not been home –

WAITER. Oh no, completely, I'm not having a go, I'm a huge fan –

ZACK. Can you just, fan of what?

ANYA. Can I see the paper?

WAITER. You can have it! I'd love you to have my paper, that'd be an honour.

Passes it to her. ZACK *intercepts it.*

ZACK. Okay, now please go away, we'd like a bit of privacy so –

WAITER. Of course, yes, say no more…

The WAITER *grabs* ZACK's *empty glass and taps it with a knife.*

Everyone, hello, *bonsoir*, sorry to interrupt, just to say we've got The Croc Madame with us here tonight, so let's maybe have a quick…

He starts clapping. And encourages the audience to join in. ANYA *slowly get to her feet and takes it in and bows.*

ZACK. Well, why are you bowing…?

WAITER. And if I could ask you all not to hassle her please and give her a bit of privacy… (*Smiles at* ZACK.) she's just turned down this gentleman's proposal so –

ZACK. Shut up! Bloody hell!

The WAITER *turns back to* ZACK.

WAITER. Sorry, yes, I was just trying to give a bit of context –

ZACK. And please just fuck off!

WAITER. Of course. Can I just say, before I do, I think it's awful what they're saying about him now. The Croc.

ANYA. What?

ZACK. What? What are they saying?

WAITER. Ugh… whipping up the rioters like that, saying he's all pro-slavery.

ZACK *furiously opens the paper,* ← *laugh + gather*

ZACK. 'Hypocroc! Money-grabbing Croc demands return of Feudal System – '

WAITER. And like, what's even wrong with that anyway?

ZACK. Oh Christ… Ivan…

ZACK *scans through the article.* /long pause

ANYA. What's the photo of me like? question – innocent

Snap blackout. The sound of a crowd baying for blood.   like
– oblivious

Building sound of baying crowd

Scene Five   Ivan – pacing the pit

IVAN/CROCODILE, *now wearing a large top hat and a tweed cravat, paces in his pit.* POPOV *stands nearby.*

IVAN/CROCODILE. Who are these people?

MR POPOV. Civil-rights nutters, animal-rights nutters, general nutters, students, a lot of students who liked you, ironically, now hate you.

IVAN/CROCODILE. Hate me ironically?

MR POPOV. No I think actually –

IVAN/CROCODILE. So get security down there –

MR POPOV. We don't have security –

IVAN/CROCODILE. I mean… for the Lord's sake, Popov!

MR POPOV. We've never needed it before.

IVAN/CROCODILE. You've never housed someone with my level of profile before. There should be at least six heavily armed heavies around me at all times.

MR POPOV. You should never have stopped doing the songs if you ask me –

IVAN/CROCODILE. People do not need songs, Popov! They need truth and… theatre –

MR POPOV. They were miles better than all this pro-serfdom stuff –

IVAN/CROCODILE. What? Who's saying that?

MR POPOV. The mob, I think, the press –

IVAN/CROCODILE. I'm not pro-serfdom!

MR POPOV. A lot of old folk are with you on that, as it goes –

IVAN/CROCODILE. They're not *with* me. I'm not *with* that. Clearly. I'm an actor! I'm all about freedom and stuff. Where are those hacks from earlier?

MR POPOV. There are a couple by the zebras –

IVAN/CROCODILE. Right! I'm going *to* clear this up –

MR POPOV. You won't get through to them though –

IVAN/CROCODILE. I will. I'll keep it simple this time. I won't do an animal story –

MR POPOV. Through the mob, I mean. They'll tear you a new one. And a big one. They're so bloody offended.

IVAN/CROCODILE. Well, can they stop being offended?

MR POPOV. I think… they don't want to –

IVAN/CROCODILE. Go and tell them to stop being offended. Popov! Quickly!

MR POPOV. Yes, alright, I'll try…

He runs to the exit and puts on a baseball cap.

PROTESTER. Traitor! Royal-bashing bastard!

IVAN/CROCODILE. Oh, shit! Popov! Help!

PROTESTER. Calling the serfs animals!

IVAN/CROCODILE. No, I didn't, I… Popov!

The PROTESTER *switches hats to becomes* POPOV *again.*

MR POPOV. I'm back, Ivan! Getting rid of him now!

He shoos the PROTESTER *out and then changes hats again to become a nobleman,* BARON BORIS BOGOLEPOV, *in a top hat.*

BORIS. Well done, laddie!

IVAN/CROCODILE. What? Thank you. Who are you?

BORIS. Baron Boris Bogelopov! Huge fan of your work! About time someone exposed this barmy emancipation bunk as a loony left-wing plot to bring down the country…

IVAN/CROCODILE. Yes, thanks, that wasn't quite what I was saying but…

He swaps hats to become MR FRAMPTON *and storms in.*

MR FRAMPTON. You bloody idiot! — without hat

IVAN/CROCODILE. What? Who's that? — with hat

MR FRAMPTON. Andrew Frampton! What did you have to go and do that for? Having a pop at business, losing our sponsorship –

IVAN/CROCODILE. I didn't pop at business, Frampton, it was about a zoo –

MR FRAMPTON. Petersham Tweed Jackets just pulled out. After your antics. Demanding that we give them the banner back. — banner falls ? — awkward silence

IVAN/CROCODILE. What about the jackets? — both looking at banner

MR FRAMPTON. And the jackets, yes.

IVAN/CROCODILE. But… I deliberately plugged tweed coats in the story…

MR FRAMPTON. Doesn't matter. You're bad news. *The Gazette* says you hate Russia –

IVAN/CROCODILE. But that's, I love Russia, I just hate the Tsar!

MR FRAMPTON. That's the same thing, you moron.

IVAN/CROCODILE. Am I in *The Gazette*? *excited – change of tone from*

ZACK *appears at the tinsel. He has a newspaper.*
~~FRAMPTON *takes down the Petersham Tweed Jackets banner*.~~

ZACK. Ivan!

IVAN/CROCODILE. Security! Frampton! *ducks down – scared*

ZACK. It's okay, it's me… it's Zack –

IVAN/CROCODILE. Oh, thank Christ you're here! I really need another coffee.

ZACK. I don't think I can go through that crowd again –

IVAN/CROCODILE. That big is it?

ZACK. Well, that livid, yes. Anya's out there now trying to stop some animal-rights people from burning this place down, Ivan –

MR FRAMPTON. Oh, bloody hell! I would absolutely hate it if they did that…! *↓ onstage   walking out = storming*

FRAMPTON *runs out ~~with the banner~~.*

IVAN/CROCODILE. Please, buddy, be a love and fetch me a coffee and copy of *The Gazette* – I need to know what these vultures are saying about me. And a coffee.

ZACK. Yeah, I've got it here. Have you not seen it?

IVAN/CROCODILE. Well, no, I've been in this room the whole time. And in this crocodile. What's it like?

He reads to IVAN *from the paper.*

ZACK. 'Big-mouth hypocrite croc-botherer, identified as jobbing actor Ivan Matveitch – ' it's not perfect…

IVAN/CROCODILE. 'Jobbing'?! What?

ZACK. That can't be the main thing you're unhappy about there –

IVAN/CROCODILE. Every actor's jobbing! That just means getting jobs…!

ZACK. 'Saw his sudden fame turn to infamy this afternoon, when he swapped his mildly diverting song-and-dance routines for a graphic and retrograde allegory attacking the Tsar's recent decision to free the serfs and comparing them to animals – '

IVAN/CROCODILE. Well, that's bang out of context!

ZACK. 'The so-called Croc Monsieur also singled out foreign tax evaders – '

IVAN/CROCODILE. Ah, right, they must be with me on that, surely – ?

ZACK. 'Despite receiving over three thousand roubles cash in ticket sales since his crocodile residency began, so far completely unaccounted for – '

IVAN/CROCODILE. What? It shouldn't be about me! Why are they focusing on me?

ZACK. 'Middle-class son of a senior civil servant, and accustomed to a life of easy privilege in St Petersburg – '

IVAN/CROCODILE. I ate cheese and turnip last night!

ZACK. 'Is, according to an ex-girlfriend, also cold-blooded in the sack – ' *laugh to himself*

IVAN/CROCODILE. I beg your sweet pardon? Which bitch said that?

ZACK. Uh… it just says… 'a dancer' –

IVAN/CROCODILE. Lies! A dancer? They're just making it up now! How can they do this to me? Have these parasites no shame? Have they no responsibility to their readers, to the truth?

ZACK (*finds a name*). Her name's 'Katya'.

[handwritten: cross from right to left past Ivan]

[handwritten star] 3

IVAN/CROCODILE. Okay, yup, no, I know who that is. Shit!

ZACK. 'After his initially headline-hogging antics, it seems like Mr Matveitch's popularity is a thing of the past – '

IVAN/CROCODILE. What? Does it really say that? *[handwritten: is he lying?]*

[handwritten: zack shows Ivan paper] ZACK. 'And maybe it's time to say "see ya later alligator".'

ZACK *closes the paper. Beat. Some shouting from outside.*

IVAN/CROCODILE. Okay, Zack, go and get Popov! We're bringing them in… I may need a bit of protection here, bud, in case it gets tasty. The croc skin should be able to soak up a bit of aggro –

ZACK. No, Ivan, please –

IVAN/CROCODILE. But I'll need you as a human shield –

ZACK. Just come out. Ivan.

IVAN/CROCODILE. What? What do you mean?

ZACK. Just come out of there. Come out and it'll all be over.

Beat.

[handwritten: 3]

IVAN/CROCODILE. I can't –

ZACK. You can. You've hollowed the thing out now. It's barely alive, you can easily climb out.

IVAN/CROCODILE. Climb?

ZACK. Slither, whatever. *[handwritten: climbs in clumbsily over front of pen]*

ZACK *manhandles the crocodile, opening the mouth.*

IVAN/CROCODILE. What are you doing? Get off!

ZACK. There's no resistance, look. It's basically dead.

IVAN *spins away from him.*

No one knows what you look like, Ivan. You can come out and just walk home. It's easy.

Beat.

Please. For all of us. This whole thing has been a bloody
nightmare.

IVAN/CROCODILE. I can see that the zoo story might have
sounded a bit anti-freedom or whatever, but that's only
because these wankers completely missed the point –

ZACK. Yeah, that's what happens –

IVAN/CROCODILE. I'll keep it simple next time, do
something even thickos can follow –

ZACK. No, Ivan, please –

IVAN/CROCODILE. I'm not stopping, man! I'm making a lot
of very good of money here – !

ZACK. So? You can't spend it, can you? You're in a crocodile.

IVAN/CROCODILE. I know that! I know I'm in a crocodile,
mate! I'm more aware of that than anyone. And being in this
crocodile is the only way I'm going to cobble together some
kind of nest egg. And, to be clear, I'm still talking about
money, I'm not literally interested in laying eggs.

ZACK. It's bad for you though, Ivan.

IVAN/CROCODILE. Hardly! Petersham's have given me four
more hacking jackets –

ZACK. It's awful for all of us.

IVAN/CROCODILE. And you got a free hanky.

ZACK. No, I know –

IVAN/CROCODILE. Everyone's a winner –

ZACK. Anya said no. Okay? I asked her to marry me and she
said no. sincere - heartfelt - hurt

IVAN/CROCODILE. That's not because of this –

ZACK. Of course it is. Please just come out, Ivan! Before
people get burnt!

IVAN/CROCODILE *takes* ZACK *by the shoulders.*

IVAN/CROCODILE. Don't panic, Zack. I know what to do now. I didn't get it before. I was naive in the extremis.

ZACK. It doesn't matter –

IVAN/CROCODILE. I shouldn't be crowbarring in the politics, it's not my forte. I need to think about my audience, about what they want –

ZACK. They don't want anything –

IVAN/CROCODILE. What drew them here in the first place. What drew me into this crocodile.

ZACK. Nothing *drew* you, it was an accident.

IVAN/CROCODILE. No. It wasn't. Nu-uh. Everything happens for a reason, Zack. Everything. I believe that.

ZACK. Yeah, and I'm sure most people who've randomly become famous for not really doing anything do too. But there's no meaning or fate here, Ivan. You're just... in a crocodile and not dead.

IVAN/CROCODILE. That's right. I'm not dead. I'm still here. And while there's breath in my gob and blood in my bod, I'm going to plough on. Give the people a show... whether they like it or not –

ZACK. It'll definitely be the latter –

IVAN/CROCODILE. In time, I know I'll win them back –

ZACK. You won't – *Building anger*

IVAN/CROCODILE. Oh, give them some credit, Zack...

ZACK. You're no good, Ivan.

Beat.

IVAN/CROCODILE. Come again?

ZACK. No matter what you do, the public won't like it. You're bad. Give up.

IVAN/CROCODILE. Is this a reverse-psychology thing?

ZACK. No.

IVAN/CROCODILE. Definitely not?

ZACK. You're a poor performer, writer, person, everything.
You have no grasp of politics, economics, law or art. Please,
God, stop.

IVAN/CROCODILE. You don't really –

ZACK. I do.

IVAN/CROCODILE. You don't know what I was going to say?

ZACK. I do think that. And I always have. You're an
embarrassment, Ivan.

IVAN *begins to splutter a bit inside the crocodile.*

Ivan? I'm sorry, I… Ivan? Are you crying in there or is
that… I don't want to say crocodile tears, but I can't really
avoid it now.

Beat.

I'm only saying this to help you –

IVAN/CROCODILE. This is you helping, is it? Mate.
Constantly stamping on my nuts, telling me I'm shit. Well,
you can bloody keep it. I don't need it. I don't need you.
There are people out there, good people, who value what I
do. What I'm about.

ZACK. I… are there?

IVAN/CROCODILE. Who, piles of them, who enjoy, if not
treasure, what I bring to the world. I overstepped the mark
earlier, I know that now. I let the attention go to my head,
and forgot what it was that people actually love about me.

ZACK. What's that?

IVAN/CROCODILE. The songs. My songs.

ZACK. What, the stupid crocodile songs – ?

IVAN/CROCODILE. *The Gazette* called them 'mildly
diverting', thank you!

ZACK. I know, I was reading it –

IVAN/CROCODILE. *The Gazette*, Zack. And in this fucked-up, dog-eat-dogshit, gang-bang of a universe, isn't a bit of diversion exactly what people need?

ZACK. No.

IVAN/CROCODILE. Isn't that the greatest service that I can provide? To make people happy. To forget their worries for one magic moment and just enjoy a man in a crocodile doing a song-and-dance number. Isn't that, when you think about it, the best thing that any of us can do? Ever? *having a moment to the audience*

ZACK. No.

IVAN/CROCODILE. If you think about it. *out of the corner of mouth* — *slightly to the side to Zack*

ZACK. I have.

IVAN/CROCODILE. If you think about it differently.

ZACK. Ivan, that animal-story stuff this afternoon is who you are. That's what you think. You've been coming out with that crap for years.

IVAN/CROCODILE. It was massively out of character –

ZACK. No it wasn't. It was weird, yes, but at least it was you. Those songs are just… they're nothing. You just want to be popular again.

IVAN/CROCODILE. How dare you!

ZACK. That's what this is, though, right?

IVAN/CROCODILE. You're disgusting. You disgust me.

ZACK. You're scared you're not going to be famous any more.

IVAN/CROCODILE. It's a little thing called 'humbility', mate.

ZACK. Well, no, it's called 'humility' –

IVAN/CROCODILE. I suggest you try it for once in your shit life.

ANYA *and* POPOV *run in.* IVAN *returns the crocodile head to normal.*

ANYA. We need to get out of here! *– really panicked*

ZACK. Really? What's happening?

ANYA. The angry mob's getting angrier and more of them –

IVAN/CROCODILE. Oh Jesus…

ANYA. They're doing punch-ups with some of your supporters.

ZACK. Supporters? Are there supporters?

IVAN/CROCODILE. Yes! You see, Zack!

MR POPOV. Yeah, all the pro-slavery lot –

IVAN/CROCODILE. Oh my God, I am not pro-slavery!

MR POPOV. And some bloody copycat idiots trying to get inside the animals –

ZACK. What? Why are they doing that?

ANYA. They think it's a way to get famous –

MR POPOV. It's an absolute zoo and a half out there! There's a boy halfway in an elk, a dead girl in a hippo, one guy's got his leg in a penguin –

IVAN/CROCODILE. Well, get them out! This is my thing –

MR POPOV. I'm not going back! That mob are mental, mate. The tinsel won't keep 'em out much longer.

ZACK. Okay, well, maybe, can we smuggle him out a back way or something?

POPOV *grabs* IVAN/CROCODILE *and starts to lead him away.*

MR POPOV. Right, yes! There's a fire exit by the flamingos.

ANYA. Well, let's, Ivan, I think we have to get a move-on…

IVAN/CROCODILE *throws them off him.* *No! cuts tone*

IVAN/CROCODILE. Bring them in!

Beat. And he walks back to his little pit.

[margin note: all luck – panic, frantic]

MR POPOV. You what? *[handwritten: ← sticks head from round corner]*

IVAN/CROCODILE. The mob. Bring them in, Popov.

ZACK. Ivan, trust me, that's a very poor idea –

IVAN/CROCODILE. And you can shut your bloody mouth, you
doubting Judas! Bring 'em in, Popov. I'm going to fix this,
right now.

POPOV *runs offstage.* ANYA *walks over to* IVAN.

ANYA. Good for you, Ivan.

MR POPOV (*off*). Right, in you come, then! Leave the placards
outside! Placards! That thing you're holding, love. It's called
a placard, yes! Come on…

*The noise of a rabble coming into the room. POPOV goes off
and immediately comes back on as SASHA. A spotlight
grows on* IVAN/CROCODILE. ZACK *and* ANYA *melt
away. The rabble noise fades.*

[handwritten margin note: not all bad ?]

IVAN/CROCODILE. Good evening. And thank you all for
coming. I know that many of you are highly offended by
some comments that were made here today, and for that I
apologise unreservedly. I am not now and never have been
pro-serfdom and it makes me sick to my guts that any of you
could think that I was. I love farmers. I respect them. I'm
proud that they've been freed. I'm not always able to express
myself, you see, I am, at heart, a silly little croc who just
wants to make you smile, but I want you to know that I love
this country. A lot. And I love the brave men and women
who work in the fields and in the factories and serve
tirelessly in our armed forces at home and overseas. We are
all the Tsar's loyal, loving subjects and now, thanks to his
grace and goodness, forever, equal. My message, ladies and
gents, is one of joy. And goodwill for all. Everything that
exists is great and everything that doesn't probably
shouldn't. I love and respect you all. And despite what the
press are saying about me, I assure you that I have no ill-will
for anything, apart from the obvious stuff like famine and
paedos. I hate them. So I'm sorry. I've let you down, I've let

[handwritten margin note: weighted - like Churchill]

[handwritten margin note: lower music chord progression]

political to cheesy

myself down, and, most of all, I've let our great emancipator,
His Royal Highness Tsar Alexander II down. Please find it in
your hearts to believe in me again. This is for you.

He starts to sing and dance.   *using tails of coat to 'dry eyes'*

Well I'm a sorry and apoloy-getic crocodile, I've got thick
green skin, but I'm still fragile. I want to cheer you up, I
want to see you smile, I'm a lovely little crocodile, that's   *fake cry*
right, I'm sunny, I'm a kinda funny, crocodile!   *— please forgive*

Freezes.   *Anya applauds*

Thank you. I love you all. Thank you so much.   *to anya*

He bows and blows kisses. SASHA, *in the audience, shouts
out.*

SASHA. Is that it?

IVAN/CROCODILE. Sorry, what?

SASHA. Is the whole 'I'm sorry' routine meant to be enough to
win back the public?

IVAN/CROCODILE. I wouldn't know about that, mate, I'm
just trying to do right by my audience and offer up a message
of love and –

SASHA. But you're just doing another song?

IVAN/CROCODILE. Yes… ideally, sorry, who are you?

SASHA. Sasha Ivkin, *Daily Record*, so what about the tax
dodge then?

IVAN/CROCODILE. I… I'd rather not talk about that –

SASHA. And the animal-cruelty stuff? What have you got to
say about that?

IVAN/CROCODILE. I, well, I think I've said what I need to
say about that… I'm concentrating on my music and –

SASHA. Okay, see you later then, Croc…

SASHA *starts to walk to the exit.* IVAN/CROCODILE
watches him go.

stood on plinth

IVAN/CROCODILE. Well no, hang on, don't go! There's more, there's, wait! I also decided some time ago, to give something back and therefore to... donate some, half of the money that I've made so far from my performances here at the zoo to... uh, crocodile-welfare... schemes, if there are any such, uh...

SASHA. I don't think there are –

IVAN/CROCODILE. To set one up then! At last! To give everyone in society, especially poor... orphans, the chance to see and admire these most marvellous creatures.

marvel at himself

SASHA. What's it called?

back looking ridiculous

IVAN/CROCODILE. It, the Ivan Matveitch Crocodile Trust will, for a mere nineteen thousand roubles, bring another crocodile to St Petersburg and... spoil it rotten, if that's, is that alright?

straight out not hesitant

SASHA. And what do you think about the kid in the elk?

IVAN/CROCODILE. The what?

SASHA. The fourteen-year-old kid who's now completely inside an elk.

IVAN/CROCODILE. Well, I wish nothing but the best for anyone trying to get into this business, but I would remind you that I was the first and therefore –

SASHA. He's only fourteen though...

SASHA *goes to make his way out.*

IVAN/CROCODILE. So? That doesn't mean that you should just... where are you going? An elk's easy! It's warm-blooded and, don't just go and gawp at some... teen! In an elk! I've got more stuff! Personal stuff.

SASHA *(stops)*. Yeah? What is it then?

IVAN/CROCODILE. Right, yes, the other, personal reason, I invited you in here today is to... share with you all, a very special moment in my life. As I'm sure you can imagine, it's both fascinating and odd living inside a crocodile, but what you maybe don't realise is that it's lonely. And I've decided that I don't want to do it alone. And that every Croc Monsieur needs, and perhaps deserves, a Croc Madame. And with that in mind –   ← sasha off to dimitri

ZACK. What? No, Ivan, stop…!

ZACK *makes his way towards the spotlight. As does* ANYA.

IVAN/CROCODILE. Not now, Zack –

ANYA. Let him speak! Go on, Ivan…

He gets down on one knee.

IVAN/CROCODILE. With that in mind, I'd like to ask my beloved Anne, light of my life, fire of my loins, to do me the honour of being my wife.

ANYA. Oh, Ivan!

DIMITRI *appears onstage and puts his camera in front of* ANYA.

DIMITRI. Anne! Over here!

ANYA *turns and poses for* DIMITRI – *overwhelmed.*

ZACK. Anya, please, this is madness, he doesn't know what he's doing –

IVAN/CROCODILE. Love is madness, Zack.

ZACK. No, but, this isn't real! It's just a show. He doesn't want this, it's just to get people's attention –

IVAN/CROCODILE. I love you, Annie.

ANYA. I love you too, Ivan.

ZACK. No, what? No you don't…

IVAN*'s hand comes out of the crocodile's mouth, holding a small red tube.*

IVAN/CROCODILE. This is some kind of… valve off one of the organs in here that, it's not an official engagement ring, but you get the idea –   doesn't fit

ANYA. Oh, wow, Ivan, I love it!

IVAN/CROCODILE. I might have to put it back if the croc
starts leaking –

ZACK. Ivan. Stop this! This is…

(*To the audience*.) Stop watching this. Can you please… this
is private…! *Downstage corner*

IVAN/CROCODILE. I know everything's been a bit bonkers
recently, Anne, but bottom line, babe, I'm just a boy, in a
crocodile, standing in front of a girl, not in a crocodile,
asking if he can marry the shit out of her. *down on knee*

ANYA. I… yes! I will!

They pose again for DIMITRI.

ZACK. But, I mean, what?

ANYA. I've never been happy with you, Zack, I'm sorry –

ZACK. Well, don't… talk about this here –

ANYA. You're holding me back, Zack, that's what you've
always done. Installing me in that flat –

ZACK. What? Installing? Do you mean… buying a flat?

ANYA. Suffocating me with cushions – *aggressive*

DIMITRI. What, really?

ZACK (*to the audience*). That's not… not literally –

ANYA. I can't be with someone with your negativity, Zack, and
height, I can't. I need to live and be free –

IVAN/CROCODILE. Amen.

ANYA. I need to be with Ivan.

ZACK. But you can't *be* with him, this is… he's in there.

IVAN *opens up the crocodile's mouth from the inside*.

IVAN/CROCODILE. I can't offer you much, Anne, but there is
room enough for two…

ANYA. Oh… really?

ZACK. Are you fucking kidding me…? *(handwritten: 3)*

(handwritten: walking round to bridge – Ivan holding her hand – really overexcited to go in croc)

IVAN/CROCODILE. I won't lie, it's not The Ritz. It's more of a fixer-upper. Right now it's a crocodile's stomach, but soon, with your delicate touch, it could be a home.

ANYA *begins to make her way to the open jaws.*

ZACK. You're not actually going in there?

ANYA. I have to, Zack. I'm sorry. This is what I was put on earth to do. *(handwritten: –up onto bridge)*

ZACK. I mean… how can that possibly be true?

(handwritten: wedding march – Owen)

ANYA *waves to the crowd. And slowly lowers herself into the crocodile.* DIMITRI *takes another photo.*

DIMITRI. Congratulations, Croc! *(handwritten: move to bottom right)*

IVAN/CROCODILE. Thank you. Thank you very much. All images will now have to be negotiated in advance, by the way. *(handwritten: talking to)*

ZACK. Can we please, Anya, this is just ridiculous now…! *(handwritten: inside the)*

ANYA *is now in the crocodile. Trumpets outside.* *(handwritten: Z look in, pit, Ivan mouth)*

DIMITRI. The Tsar! The Tsar's here! *(handwritten: ↑ music)*

DIMITRI *runs offstage.*

ZACK. Yup, right, of course he is – *(handwritten: crumple into a chair – fully aghast)*

IVAN/CROCODILE. Your Majesty!

The CROCODILE *kneels as the* TSAR *enters slowly* (POPOV *in enormous crown and cape*). *He extends his hand for the* CROCODILE *to kiss.*

We are truly honoured, sire. *(handwritten: pull hand from Ivan)*

TSAR ALEXANDER II. My dear Russians. Although I am your ▪ divinely ordained leader, I stand here today as a fan.

IVAN/CROCODILE. Oh wow… My Liege… *(handwritten: steps in front of Ivan) stands in front of Ivan*

TSAR ALEXANDER II. Let no one say that the Tsar does not take an interest in the popular cultural phenomena of the age. I am, like you, a huge supporter of whatever it is that is going on here that you all like so much.

IVAN/CROCODILE. It's mainly song-and-dance numbers, Your Highness – *peeking out from behind tsar*

TSAR ALEXANDER II. And I should add, that I have been truly moved by this crocodile's charming message of equality and patriotism. We are all equal in this country now, the final barriers of class and privilege have been cast aside and we all have the full freedom to flourish in any way that we see fit.

tsar cuts him off hand in front of face in front of Ivan

IVAN/CROCODILE. Hear hear! *irritated by Ivan – eye role*

TSAR ALEXANDER II. And let this talking animal's humble plea for joy and love be a beacon to you all to seek *put down Insidious* satisfaction and peace in your own lives, and not to question or complain or succumb to the poison of petty envy, but to fight these malignant political forces at work in our country, that wear the mask of common good but bring only destruction and chaos. We will look after you. We will entertain you. We will give you all that you need. Arise, Sir Crocodile, and let Russia salute you.

insidious to the audience direct

IVAN/CROCODILE. At once, Your Majesty.

The CROCODILE *stands.*   *to audience*

TSAR ALEXANDER II. In pleasing my people, you please me. I thank you for your support, and now, hereafter, pledge you mine.

turn and walk back to Ivan

The TSAR *kneels before the* CROCODILE *and kisses his hand.*

Trumpets. The CROCODILE *turns to face the audience. Regal. Defiant.*   *Drawn out fanfare*

Blackout.

Properly arrogant last look